ALL TALK

Problem Solving for New Students of English

JANN HUIZENGA
City University of New York

MARIA THOMAS-RUŽIĆ
University of Colorado at Boulder

HEINLE & HEINLE PUBLISHERS
A Division of Wadsworth, Inc.
Boston, Massachusetts 02116

COVER ART: Brian Karas

ART AND ILLUSTRATIONS: Steven Mach, Brian Karas, Paige Billin-Frye, Precision Graphics.

PHOTO CREDITS: Jann Huizenga: pp. 1, 8, 9, 10, 35, 39, 45, 74, 95(c), 103; Kim Crowley: pp. 13, 16, 19, 63, 64, 65, 70, 95(a,h); Lee Hagen: pp. 8, 10, 35, 36; Ranko Ružić: pp. 34, 60, 61, 81; National Archives: p. 35; Courtesy John R. Shrader and National Archives: p. 36; Courtesy John Hendry and National Archives: p. 36; The Library of Congress: pp. 41(a), 109; Reuters/Bettmann Newsphotos: p. 41(e); The Bettmann Archive: pp. 41(k), 109; Linda Huizenga: pp. 41(i), 44; Joel Huizenga: p. 74; Steamboat Springs: p. 83; Dolly Huizenga: p. 83; Egyptian Tourist Authority: p. 83; French Government Tourist Office: p. 88; Yankee Stadium: p. 95(f); Chicago Convention & Tourism Bureau: p. 95(d); Cedar Point: p. 95(e,g); Chicago Photographic Company: p. 95(b); American Cancer Society: p. 114.

ISBN: 0-8384-3979-9

Heinle & Heinle Publishers is a division of Wadsworth, Inc.

10 9 8 7 6 5 4 3

ABOUT THIS BOOK

All Talk is an introductory text for adult and young-adult learners of English as a Second Language (ESL) or English as a Foreign Language (EFL) who are beginning to express themselves in English. *All Talk* uses decision-making tasks to encourage meaningful and purposeful oral practice in English. It can be used on its own in an oral skills course or in tandem with *Writing Workout* (Heinle & Heinle, 1990) in a writing and oral skills program. Its fifteen self-contained lessons provide material for approximately thirty to forty-five class hours (two to three hours per lesson), depending on the proficiency of the students and the purposes of the course. If full use is made of the various extension activities in the GRAMMAR APPENDIX and INSTRUCTOR'S NOTES, however, *All Talk* provides material for a longer course.

TOPICS

All Talk engages new to intermediate users of English in challenging and fun problems for discussion. The text offers topics of adult relevance and high human interest while at the same time recognizing students' limited linguistic and communicative skills in English. Its fifteen problem-solving activities have been selected to provide a wide variety of provocative (but not inflammatory) topics. It should be noted that some topics will be better suited than others to a given class, and the instructor (perhaps with help from students) should feel free to pick and choose among them. Some problems engage students in down-to-earth, practical issues of everyday life (for example, "Divide the Household Chores," "Work Out a Family Budget," and "Decide on Appropriate Salaries"). In these lessons, students play familiar roles such as parent, child, or worker. Other lessons involve students in hypothetical or fantasy situations (for example, "Rent a Vacation Home," "Design a Dream Home," and "Play Matchmaker"). These lessons challenge students' imaginations with novel roles such as lottery winner, architect, or dating agency employee. In still another type of lesson, students solve community and global problems ("Improve Your Hometown," "Organize a Sports Schedule," and "Save the Planet," for example) and play roles of town leader, community member, or environmental planner.

The inclusion of both familiar and unfamiliar contexts and roles and of both real and hypothetical situations has been motivated by a "whole learner" view of adult ESL/EFL students, in which they are believed to profit not only from activities that relate directly to their everyday experiences but also from those that challenge their imaginations and put them in novel situations.

UNIQUE FEATURES

All Talk has several special features that make it unique.

• *Accessibility to beginners*

All Talk is unique among ESL/EFL discussion books in that it makes problem-solving tasks accessible to students who have very limited oral skills. This accessibility is achieved by the careful language buildup preceding each group problem-solving task. That is, each lesson lays out a sequence of small steps that prepares students to express themselves on the topic at hand. This preparatory language work includes vocabulary study, grammar work, and work with functional expressions. The text thus balances a focus on accuracy (in the language buildup) with a focus on fluency (in the problem-solving task).

• *Focus on critical thinking skills*

Critical thinking skills are fostered along with language and communication skills. Each lesson includes a section entitled "Stop and Think," which has students practice such skills as comparing, classifying, evaluating, and ranking.

• *Flexibility*

A high degree of flexibility is provided in the organization of the book, which contains five thematic units with three lessons apiece. These fifteen lessons can be done in any sequence, perhaps depending on topics that are being covered in class or particular interests of students. Alternatively, for instructors using *Writing Workout,* units or portions of units can be used sequentially to coordinate with the same five thematic units in *Writing Workout.* Note that Lessons 1, 2, 4, and 5 have the relatively easiest activities in terms of language, while the third lesson of each unit (Lessons 3, 6, 9, 12, and 15) is more challenging. The remaining lessons fall somewhere in between.

A self-correcting GRAMMAR APPENDIX provides additional flexibility. These grammar activities can be assigned to students who need work in a particular area. Because students can correct their own work, the activities are ideal as independent in-class activities or as homework assignments.

An ANSWER APPENDIX for selected activities in the text gives instructors the option to do whole-class correction or to have students check their answers on their own.

INSTRUCTOR'S NOTES, easily accessible at the back of the text, offer a variety of options for the activities in each lesson. They also include "Extension Activities," quiz ideas, and suggestions for ways to get at cross-cultural issues.

• *Emphasis on visuals*

Photographs and illustrations are liberally used as pedagogical devices. First, the rich visual context is used to provide ready access to the topic of each lesson. It is also used to give beginning-level students quick keys to the meanings of words. And, finally, photographs and illustrations serve as jumping-off points for many of the discussions in the text. A focus on visuals prevents the new learner of English from becoming overburdened with the written word.

ORGANIZATION OF LESSONS

Each lesson is composed of these sections: *Warming Up, Word Power, (Sentence Power), Stop and Think, Talk It Over,* and *Writing Review.*

Warming Up presents photographs and illustrations to introduce the topic of the lesson and to draw students' own interests and backgrounds to the topic. A limited number of relevant vocabulary items are introduced here. The *Warming Up* task can be done individually or in pairs, followed by a whole-class check or discussion. Words and phrases generated by students can be put on the board and incorporated into the activity.

Word Power presents words and phrases that are necessary for the culminating problem-solving activity. It also provides practice with these new vocabulary items. Instructors should allow students to hear and practice the pronunciation of the new vocabulary before assigning the task. In cases where word meanings are not clarified by visuals, students can be encouraged to pool resources with fellow students or to use their dictionaries. This activity is suitable for individual or pair work and can be followed by a whole-class check or discussion.

Sentence Power provides practice with a grammatical structure that students will need to use in the problem-solving activity. Vocabulary from the lesson is reinforced here.

Stop and Think guides students in thinking critically about the topic at hand. The activities in this section require students to compare items, consider good and bad sides of things, read between the lines, evaluate or rank-order items, clarify personal opinions, and so on. While encouraging students to begin formulating a personal opinion about the upcoming problem, this section also gives students more practice with the language they will need to use in the discussion.

Talk It Over presents the problem-solving task for each lesson. First, the situation and roles are clarified, and a few basic language functions relevant to the task are provided in the "Helpful Language" boxes. These functional phrases should be modeled and practiced before students embark on the problem-solving task, which is designed for small groups. A time limit for arriving at a consensus should be announced before students get started. A limit of ten to fifteen minutes is suitable for most problems in *All Talk.* Finally, the text suggests regrouping the whole class for a debriefing of the problem, that is, a whole-class exchange of solutions and ideas. Five to ten minutes will usually suffice for this part of the activity, but high student involvement may signal that more time should be allowed. The INSTRUCTOR'S NOTES offer a number of suggestions on how to group students, set time limits, and ensure that members interact.

Writing Review provides a variety of consolidation tasks such as filling out forms, writing postcards, and making lists. These activities give students the opportunity to review words and phrases as well as ideas that have come up in the lesson. The activity can be done in class if desired; it is also ideal for homework.

ACKNOWLEDGMENTS

We express our appreciation to students and colleagues in the MA in TESOL Program at Hunter College, City University of New York, and at the International English Center and the Department of Linguistics at the University of Colorado at Boulder, who contributed in many different ways to this project. We extend special thanks to Jean Engler, Director of the International English Center at the University of Colorado, for her invaluable support for this long-distance effort. We thank our reviewers, Rosemary Chavez, Leann Howard, Donna Jurich, Christine Larsen, Luz Parades Lono, Kathleen Santopietro, and Julia A. Spinthourakis for their excellent and thorough comments which helped us address weaknesses in early drafts. Also, thanks to Clare Baird for her technical assistance and to our students and friends who helped us out with photography. We sincerely thank our editors Roseanne Mendoza, Mary Jane Maples, Elaine Goldberg, and Anita Portugal for their enthusiasm, expertise, and patience.

We have some personal thanks to extend as well. Spouses Kim Crowley and Ranko Ružić contributed some great ideas and photos. We thank Luka Ružić for his insightful critical feedback throughout the drafting of the text. Josip Ružić also helped in his own special way. Jann is grateful to her parents, Dolly and John, and Mia thanks her parents, Lydia and Lloyd Thomas, for their grandparenting and nurturing. The authors are grateful for a decade-long friendship and collaboration dating back to the old days in Sarajevo.

CONTENTS

Home Sweet Home

1 **IMPROVE YOUR HOMETOWN**
   You are community leaders in a very small town. You must decide what new facilities your town needs.

2 **RENT A VACATION HOME**
   You've won the lottery! You and your friends or family are taking a ten-day vacation. But which vacation home will you rent?

*3 **DESIGN A DREAM HOME**
   Many of us already have an image of our "perfect" home. Here is your chance to design one—either for yourself or for a Hollywood star.

   *more challenging

HELPFUL LANGUAGE REFERENCE

The following expressions may be helpful in your discussions. Refer to them as needed.

AGREEING	DISAGREEING
Yes, I think you're right.	*I don't agree.*
I agree.	*I disagree.*
That's a good point.	*I don't think so.*

GIVING FEEDBACK (showing you are listening)

I see your point.
OK.
Right.
Uh-huh.

ASKING FOR CLARIFICATION

What do you mean?
What did you say?
Could you explain that?

BRINGING SOMEONE INTO THE CONVERSATION

*What do **you** think about this?*
*What's **your** opinion?*
Do you agree (with me, with John)?

MAKING A NEW SUGGESTION

Let's talk about _____ .
Let's think about _____ .
How about _____ ?
What about _____ ?

COMING TO A CONSENSUS

Does everybody agree?
Let's decide.
We have to decide now.
What's our final decision?

1 ► Improve Your Hometown

WARMING UP: Looking at facilities in town

1-A Look at these places. Match each with a name.

c a library   e an art museum   h a swimming pool
g a video arcade   F a movie theater   c a park
b a cafe   g a zoo (Tireb)

1-B Do you like these places? Which ones? Tell a partner.

I like art museums and _____.

I don't like zoos or _____.

WORD POWER: Things to do in your free time

1-C   Fill in the blanks with your own ideas or use verbs from the box. (Use a dictionary if necessary.)

1.   In an art museum, you can _see_ _paintings_ and _relax_ .

2.   At a zoo, you can _have fun_ and _watch the monkeys_

3.   In a video arcade, you can _play games_ and _have fun_.

4.   In a park, you can _enjoy nature_ and _see the tree_.

5.   In a cafe, you can _meet friends_ and _watch people_ .

6.   In a library, you can _forget your troubles_ and _read magazines_

7.   In a movie theater, you can _see the movies_ and _relax_ .

8.   At a pool, you can _swim_ and _see people_ .

> swim
> jog
> enjoy nature
> learn something new
> relax
> see paintings
> meet friends
> forget your troubles
> keep fit
> escape from reality
> read magazines
> watch people
> have fun
> play games
> watch the monkeys
> watch films

1-D   Role-play with a partner. Invite your partner to three places. Your partner will refuse each suggestion. Follow the model. Then change roles.

> Partner 1:   66 Let's go to the pool! We can swim. 99
> Partner 2:   66 I don't feel like swimming today. 99

1-E   INDEPENDENT GRAMMAR STUDY: *Can/Can't*
Turn to page 102 in the Grammar Appendix.

STOP AND THINK: Identifying who will benefit

1-F   Form a group of three or four. Imagine you are community leaders of a very small town. There are not many things to do in your town, but the town has just collected enough tax moneys to build *three* new places.

With your group, decide who will benefit most from each place below if it is built. Put a check (√) next to your answer(s) for each place.

zoo
- √ children
- √ teenagers
- √ adults
- _____ the elderly

art museum
- 4 children
- 2 teenagers
- 1 √ adults
- 3 the elderly

park
- 2 children
- _____ teenagers
- / adults
- / the elderly

library
- / children
- / teenagers
- / adults
- _____ the elderly

movie theater
- / children
- / teenagers
- / adults
- _____ the elderly

cafe
- _____ children
- _____ teenagers
- 1 adults
- 2 the elderly

video arcade
- / children
- / teenagers
- / adults
- _____ the elderly

swimming pool
- / children
- 1 teenagers
- 1 adults
- 1 the elderly

TALK IT OVER: Improving your hometown

1-G   What will your town build? Discuss the issue with your group and together choose *three* places from page 3.

HELPFUL LANGUAGE

EXPRESSING AN OPINION AND GIVING REASONS
In my opinion, (a pool) is important.
I think our town needs (a pool) because (everybody likes to swim).

AGREEING
Yes, I think you're right.
Yes, I agree with you.
Absolutely!

DISAGREEING
I don't know. I think (a park) is more important.
I don't agree. We need (a park).

Write your group's choices here.

1. _____.

2. _____.

3. _____.

1-H Complete this sentence with your group.

We think a/an _____ is the most

important place to build because _____

_____

_____ .

1-I Write your group's choices on the board and give your reasons to the class. Do the other groups agree with you?

WRITING REVIEW: A short memo

1-J Write a memo to the mayor to explain your group's decision. Use your own paper and the model below.

Write the names of your group members and today's date.

Write the names of the places you want to build.

Give your reasons. Who will use each place? What can they do there?

Memorandum

TO: Mayor Lee
FROM:
RE: New facilities for town
DATE:

After much discussion, we have reached the conclusion that our town needs the following three facilities: a/an _____ ,
a/an _____ , and a/an _____
_____ .

Please note our reasons below. _____

_____

_____

_____

_____

_____

_____

2 Rent a Vacation Home

WARMING UP: Looking at vacation homes

2-A   Congratulations! You've just won the lottery. The first thing you want to do is take a vacation. You see these houses for rent in the newspaper. Match the words below with the houses.

big	old	simple	peaceful
small	modern	luxurious	noisy

In the country

In the mountains

In town

On the beach

2-B   Do you prefer the beach house, the country house, the mountain house, or the house in town? Why? Tell a partner. Where can you swim? take walks? ride a horse?

Tarea   Escribir mi casa de los sunos.

WORD POWER: Features of a great vacation house

2-C   Ji Young dreams about taking a vacation in a home like this.
What are its nice features? Make sentences below with *It has _____*.

(a nice view)

window

tree

flowers

lawn   porch

horse

beach

pool

terrace

1.   It has a nice beach   .

2.   It has many big trees   .

3.   _____ .

4.   _____ .

5.   _____ .

6.   _____ .

7.   _____ .

8.   _____ .

2-D   **INDEPENDENT GRAMMAR STUDY:** *There is/There are*
Turn to page 103 in the Grammar Appendix.

2-E   Rewrite the sentences in 2–C using *There is* or *There are*. Use your
own paper.

STOP AND THINK: Identifying positive and negative sides

2-F   Would you like to spend your vacation in any of these houses?
With a partner, write down two or three positive features and one negative
feature of each house.

Positive (+)	*Negative (−)*

1. It has a beach . It doesn't have trees .
   It has a porch . It's small .
   There's a good view .

2. It has a one . It doesn't have
   horse, . a beach,
   It has many trees
   It has a one child
   It has a big house

3. It has a large grass It doesn't have .
   It has a big country. a horse.
   house I doesn't have
   . a beach
   It doesn't have a tree

4. It has a fountain It doesn't have a .
   It has a big farmhouse horse,
   It has a big window
   It has a big tree

TALK IT OVER: Renting a vacation house

2-G   Form a group of three or four. You are a family or a group of friends. With your lottery money, you are going to rent one of the houses on page 8 for ten days. (All rents are the same.) Together, choose one.

HELPFUL LANGUAGE

MAKING SUGGESTIONS
Let's rent the house in town. It has a pool.
We can swim.
The restaurants are close.

EXPRESSING PREFERENCES AND GIVING REASONS
I prefer the country house because there is _____ .

I like the mountain house. It has _____ , and we can _____ .

When you finish your discussion, circle your final choice.

the beach house

the country house

the mountain house

the house in town

2-H   With your group, complete these sentences.

We want to rent _____ because

_____ .

We didn't like _____ because

_____ .

2-I   Discuss your group's choice with the class. Do the other groups agree with you?

WRITING REVIEW: A friendly postcard

2-J   Write a postcard to a friend and describe your vacation house. For a sample postcard, see page 124 in the Answer Appendix.

Sunburst Graphics, 105 Eastland Avenue, Midway, CA 99999

U.S.A. 19¢

Sunburst Graphics © 1991

3 Design a Dream Home

3–A   In which room or rooms of a house can you usually find these things? Discuss your ideas with a partner.

We can usually find _____ in the _____ or in the _____ .

bathroom
bedroom
closet
dining room
family room
hallway
kitchen
living room

an umbrella

a telephone

pens and pencils

a remote control for the TV

medicine

a picture

a dustpan

a book

scissors

toilet paper

a clock

13

WORD POWER: Words that tell location

3-B   Look at this floor plan. Fill in the blanks below with the correct word or phrase from the box. Check your answers on page 125 in the Answer Appendix.

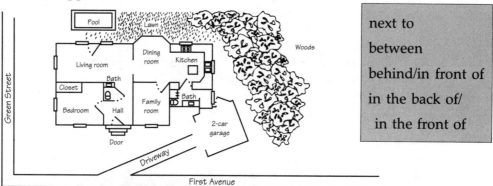

next to

between

behind/in front of

in the back of/

in the front of

1.   The pool is _____behind_____ the house.

2.   The dining room is _____ the kitchen and the living room.

3.   The family room is _____ the house.

4.   The bedroom is _____ the hallway.

5.   The driveway is _____ the house.

6.   The dining room is _____ the house.

3-C   *The kitchen looks out on the woods* means that the kitchen looks toward the woods. Fill in these blanks with the correct phrases from the box. Check your answers on page 125 in the Answer Appendix.

the pool

First Avenue

the woods

Green Street

1.   The kitchen looks out on _____the woods_____.

2.   The family room looks out on _____.

3.   The living room looks out on _____

and _____.

4.   The big bathroom looks out on _____.

5.   The bedroom looks out on _____ and

_____.

STOP AND THINK: Comparing and evaluating houses

3-D　　Compare these house floor plans. Answer the questions at the right and think about which house you prefer.

How many closets are there? _____
bathrooms? _____ bedrooms? _____

Relative to the size of the house, what
size is the kitchen? _____ *
living room? _____ dining room? _____

Write S (small), M (medium), or L (large).

How many closets are there? _____
bathrooms? _____ bedrooms? _____

What size is the kitchen? _____
living room? _____ dining room? _____

How many closets are there? _____
bathrooms? _____ bedrooms? _____

What size is the kitchen? _____
living room? _____ dining room? _____

3-E　　Which house do you prefer? Why? What's wrong with the other houses? Tell a partner.

> Partner 1:　❝ Which house do you prefer? ❞
> Partner 2:　❝ I prefer house B. It has _____.
> 　　　　　　House C doesn't have _____. ❞

3-F　　**INDEPENDENT GRAMMAR STUDY:** *(It) has/(It) doesn't have*
Turn to page 104 in the Grammar Appendix.

TALK IT OVER: Designing a dream home

3-G   Choose option A (this page) or option B (next page).

OPTION A: Form a group of two or three. You are a team of well-known architects. Sally Star (an actress who also makes exercise videotapes) wants you to design a new Hollywood home for her. Draw a floor plan of the house in the lot below.

Here is some information about Sally.

- She hates street noise.
- She loves a view of water.
- She has many dinner parties.
- She likes to exercise.
- She is president of Californians for Clean Air.
- She wants a one-story house.
- She has two children, Jill (5) and Bill (9).
- Her children like to have friends over.
- Her parents live with her.
- She has many, many clothes.

HELPFUL LANGUAGE

MAKING SUGGESTIONS
Let's put her bedroom here next to the pond.
Let's make a big closet in her bedroom.
How about a bathroom in her bedroom?
The kitchen should look out on the street/pond.

EXPRESSING NEED
She needs a big dining room.
She needs a family room for the kids.
She doesn't need a large kitchen.

Hollywood Boulevard

Green Pond

OPTION B: On your own, design and draw a floor plan of *your* dream house below. Think about these questions.

- How many bedrooms do you want/need?
- How many bathrooms do you want/need?
- Do you need a big kitchen?
- Do you want a family room?
- Do you want an extra room for a hobby or sport?
- Where will you put each room? Why?

 Show your design to a partner when you finish. Explain why this house is perfect for you.

DRAW OUTLINES OF EACH ROOM HERE.

☐ = 1 square meter (10.8 square feet)

WRITING REVIEW: Project notes

3-H   Fill in these project notes about the house you designed. For sample notes, check page 126 in the Answer Appendix.

Write your
name(s) here.

Put a number
here.

Mention any
special feature
such as size or
location here.

PROJECT:

ARCHITECT(S):

☐ BEDROOMS
Notes: _____
_____

☐ BATHROOMS
Notes: _____
_____

☐ – CAR GARAGE
Notes: _____
_____

☐ KITCHEN
Notes: _____
_____

☐ CLOSETS
Notes: _____
_____

☐ FAMILY ROOM
Notes: _____
_____

☐ DINING ROOM
Notes: _____
_____

☐ LIVING ROOM
Notes: _____
_____

☐ OTHER (a)
Notes: _____
_____

☐ OTHER (b)
Notes: _____
_____

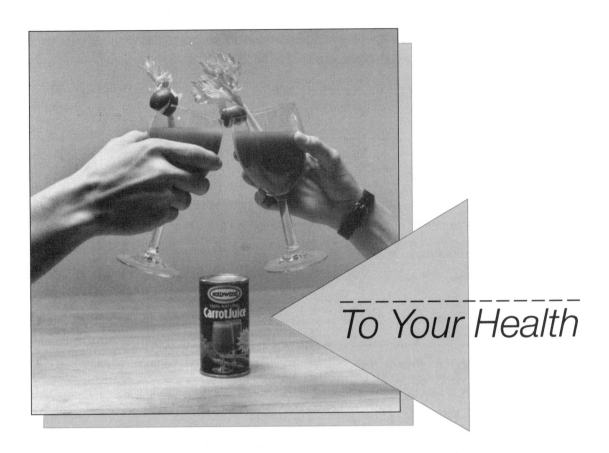

To Your Health

4   **PLAN YOUR PARTY MENU**
Your class is having a party! You need to plan a dinner menu that everyone will like.

5   **ORGANIZE A SPORTS SCHEDULE**
You run a community sports center. You must organize the sports schedule for fall.

*6   **SAVE THE PLANET**
Your group is a team of environmental experts.
You have to choose a project to work on. Which environmental problem is the most serious?

*more challenging

HELPFUL LANGUAGE REFERENCE

The following expressions may be helpful in your discussions. Refer to them as needed.

AGREEING	DISAGREEING
Yes, I think you're right.	*I don't agree.*
I agree.	*I disagree.*
That's a good point.	*I don't think so.*

GIVING FEEDBACK (showing you are listening)
I see your point.
OK.
Right.
Uh-huh.

ASKING FOR CLARIFICATION
What do you mean?
What did you say?
Could you explain that?

BRINGING SOMEONE INTO THE CONVERSATION
*What do **you** think about this?*
*What's **your** opinion?*
Do you agree (with me, with John)?

MAKING A NEW SUGGESTION
Let's talk about _____ .
Let's think about _____ .
How about _____ ?
What about _____ ?

COMING TO A CONSENSUS
Does everybody agree?
Let's decide.
We have to decide now.
What's our final decision?

4 Plan Your Party Menu

WARMING UP: Looking over a menu

4-A   Do you like to eat out? What's your favorite meal? Look at the dinner menu from Ponte's Restaurant. Can you find the names of the foods pictured below?

Ponte's
CONTINENTAL CUISINE

APPETIZERS	
Chicken soup	1.25
Shrimp cocktail	3.50
Chips with cheese dip	2.00

ENTREES	
Fried chicken	6.00
Steak with onions	7.00
Broiled fish of the day	7.00
Vegetarian stew with rice	5.00
Spaghetti with tomato sauce	5.50

VEGETABLES	
Baked potato	1.25
French fries	1.25
Corn	1.50
Green beans	1.50

DESSERTS	
Cherry pie	2.00
Chocolate cake	2.50
Ice cream	1.75
Strawberries with cream	2.50

BEVERAGES	
Mineral water	1.25
Soft drinks	1.00
Juice (apple or orange)	2.00
Coffee	1.00
Tea	1.00

a   b   c   d   e   f

g   h   i   j   k   l   m

4-B   Which of these foods do you really like? Which don't you like? Tell a partner.

I really like _____.

I don't like _____.

WORD POWER: Dollars and cents phrases

4–C   Work with a partner. One of you will look at this page and ask about the prices of six foods below. The other will look at the menu on page 21 and give the prices. Then change roles.

> Partner 1: **❝ How much is the coffee? ❞**
> Partner 2: **❝ It's a dollar. ❞**
>
> Partner 1: **❝ How much are the french fries? ❞**
> Partner 2: **❝ They're a dollar twenty-five. ❞**

SAY: $1.00 = a/one dollar $2.25 = two twenty-five
       $1.25 = a dollar twenty-five $2.50 = two fifty
       $1.50 = a dollar fifty $3.00 = three dollars
       $2.00 = two dollars $3.25 = three twenty-five

Price $2.50

4–D   **INDEPENDENT GRAMMAR STUDY: Singular and Plural Nouns**
Turn to page 105 in the Grammar Appendix.

STOP AND THINK: Considering the taste and healthfulness of foods

4-E   Which foods from the menu do you prefer? Write your favorite foods from each group. Then ask a partner about his or her choices.

Example: *Which appetizer do you prefer?*

	YOU	*YOUR PARTNER*
Appetizer		
Entree		
Vegetable		
Dessert		
Beverage		

Do you and your partner like to eat any of the same things? If so, which ones?

4-F   People today are talking a lot about eating and health. Can you find foods on the menu that are good for you? Can you find foods that are *not* so good for you (especially when you eat a lot of them)? Work with a partner and make two lists.

GOOD FOR YOU	*NOT SO GOOD FOR YOU*

TALK IT OVER: Planning your party menu

4-G   Form a group of three or four. Your class will have a party at Ponte's, a good restaurant near school. You need to choose *one* meal for everyone; in other words, everyone will eat the same things. The cost per student should not be more than $10.50. Ponte's will provide free beverages. Together, decide on the menu and write it below. (See Ponte's menu on page 21.)

HELPFUL LANGUAGE

EXPRESSING OPINIONS ABOUT FOOD
_____ *is good./* _____ *isn't good.*   *It's good for you./It's not good for you.*
It's healthy./It's unhealthy.   *It's expensive./It's not expensive.*

EXPRESSING LIKES, DISLIKES, AND PREFERENCES
Everyone likes it.   *I don't like it!* _____ *is much better.*
I love it.   *I like* _____ *better than* _____ *.*

MAKING SUGGESTIONS
Let's order _____ *.*
How about _____ *?*

Party Menu

Cost per student _____

4–H   Write your group's menu on the board. Which foods on the menu are most popular with the class? Which foods are unpopular?

WRITING REVIEW: A menu

4–I   Arrange these foods on the menu below.

curried chicken	fried rice with shrimp	broccoli
apple pie	carrots	Cuban black beans
mashed potatoes	cheesecake	shrimp cocktail
tomato soup	banana cream pie	iced tea
chopped steak	spaghetti with clam sauce	vegetarian chili
strawberry ice cream	apple juice	mineral water
soft drinks	soup of the day	

Menu

APPETIZERS
tomato soup

VEGETABLES

DESSERTS

ENTREES

BEVERAGES

See page 127 in the Answer Appendix to check your work.

5 ▸ Organize a Sports Schedule

WARMING UP: Looking at sports

5-A   Can you guess what sports these pictures represent? Match the names of the sports with the pictures.

baseball   tennis   jogging/running
dancing   basketball   volleyball
Ping-Pong   soccer   swimming
ice skating

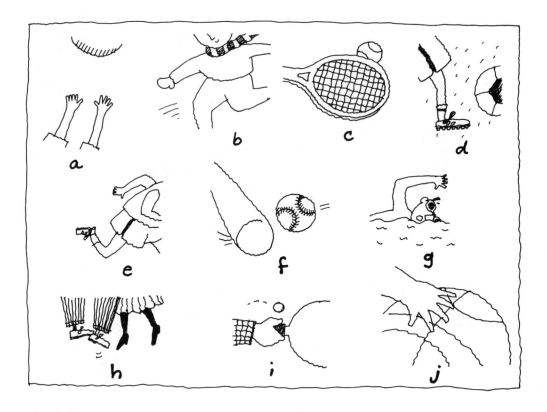

5-B   What is your favorite sport? Do you participate in this sport, or do you watch it on TV?

WORD POWER: Sports phrases

5-C Follow the model and interview a partner about his or her sports habits. Fill out the questionnaire with the information that your partner gives you. Then change roles.

Partner 1:	66 **Do you walk?** 99
Partner 2:	66 **Yes, often./sometimes./but rarely.** 99
	66 **No, never.** 99

??????? SPORTS Questionnaire ???????

Do you	OFTEN	SOMETIMES	RARELY	NEVER
—walk?	☐	☐	☐	☐
—jog?	☐	☐	☐	☐
—ride a bike?	☐	☐	☐	☐
—dance?	☐	☐	☐	☐
—play Ping-Pong?	☐	☐	☐	☐
—play basketball?	☐	☐	☐	☐
—play soccer?	☐	☐	☐	☐
—play volleyball?	☐	☐	☐	☐
—play tennis?	☐	☐	☐	☐
—play baseball?	☐	☐	☐	☐
—do aerobics?	☐	☐	☐	☐
—swim?	☐	☐	☐	☐
—ice-skate?	☐	☐	☐	☐
—lift weights?	☐	☐	☐	☐
—do karate?	☐	☐	☐	☐
—_____? (other)	☐	☐	☐	☐

Be ready to tell the class something about your partner's habits.

Example: *My partner often walks, but she never jogs. She sometimes swims.*

5-D **INDEPENDENT GRAMMAR STUDY: Simple Present**
Turn to page 106 in the Grammar Appendix.

STOP AND THINK: Classifying sports

5-E   Sports can be classified into two categories—individual sports and team sports. (Team sports require at least two people to play.) Classify these sports into the two categories.

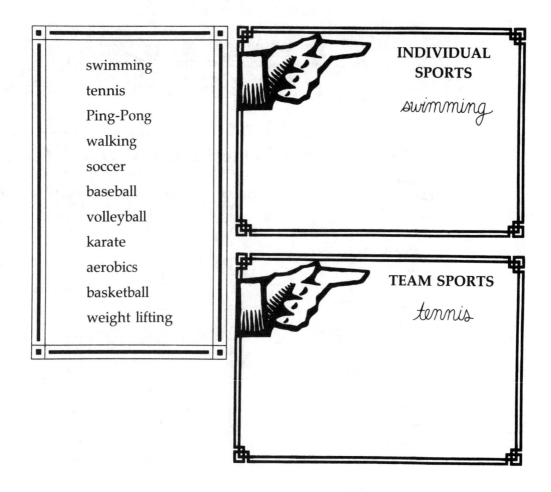

swimming
tennis
Ping-Pong
walking
soccer
baseball
volleyball
karate
aerobics
basketball
weight lifting

INDIVIDUAL SPORTS

swimming

TEAM SPORTS

tennis

See page 128 in the Answer Appendix to check your work.

5-F   Which sports are popular in your country with children? teenagers? adults? families? people over sixty-five?

SENTENCE POWER: Using *like/don't like* + infinitive

5-G   Complete these sentences according to your own experience. Use the verbs from this list and follow the model.

do karate	swim	play Ping-Pong
do aerobics	walk	play soccer
lift weights	play volleyball	play basketball
dance	play tennis	

1. Most children I know *like to swim* _____ ,

   but *they don't like to lift weights* _____ .

2. Many teenagers I know _____ ,

   but _____ .

3. Most women I know _____ ,

   but _____ .

4. Many men I know _____ ,

   but _____ .

5. Most families I know _____ ,

   but _____ .

6. Many people over sixty-five I know _____ ,

   but _____ .

Share your ideas with the class.

TALK IT OVER: Organizing a sports schedule

5-H   Form a group of three or four. Your group runs the community sports center. You must plan the evening schedule for fall. Decide which two sports will be offered each night—one individual sport and one team sport. Fill in the schedule.

HELPFUL LANGUAGE

MAKING SUGGESTIONS
Why don't we have (tennis) on Sundays?
Let's have (tennis) on Sundays.

GIVING REASONS
It's popular with (women).   *(Women) like (tennis).*
It's fun for (women).   *Lots of (women) play.*

DISAGREEING
It isn't popular with them.   *It's too boring/strenuous.*
They don't like to play.   *I think they prefer _____.*
Not many (women) like it.

FALL HEALTH AND RECREATION PROGRAM

Sundays	*Mondays*	*Tuesdays*	*Wednesdays*	*Thursdays*	*Fridays*	*Saturdays*
Women's Night 7:00 – 9:00	Men's Night 7:00 – 9:00	Children's Night 5:00 – 7:00	Family Night 6:00 – 8:00	Over 65 Night 7:00 – 9:00	—	Teen Night 7:00 – 9:00
	I N D I V I D U A L		S P O R T S		C L O S E D	
	T E A M S P O R T S					

5–I   Your instructor may ask you to put your schedule on the board.

WRITING REVIEW: An information sheet

5–J   Your local community sports center wants information about your sports activities so the center can plan its schedule. Fill in the blanks.

SPORTS CENTER INFORMATION SHEET

Please help us plan our schedule by answering these questions.

1. What is your favorite sport?

   _____

2. How often do you play or do this sport?

   _____

3. Why do you enjoy it?

   _____

   _____

4. As a young girl or boy, which sports did you like?

   _____

   _____

5. Is there a new sport that you would like to try?

   _____

   _____

6 Save the Planet

WARMING UP: Looking at the dangers we face

The earth is in danger. We are polluting the air, water, and land. We are wasting energy and other resources. We are killing off some plants and animals.

6-A Work with a partner. Circle the things that pollute our planet. Then discuss your ideas with the class.

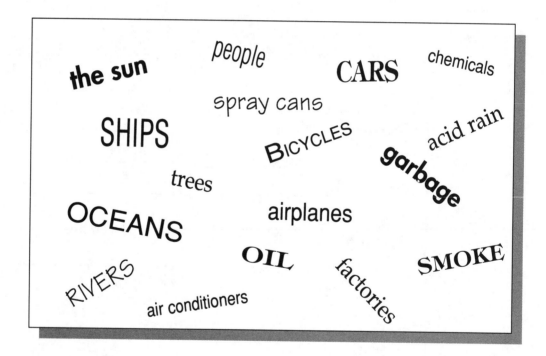

6-B Can you think of some other things that are bad for the environment?

WORD POWER: Names of pollution sources

6-C Look at these causes of pollution. Can you add others?

Some causes of air pollution:

factories   cars   _____

                                         (your idea)

Some causes of water pollution:

oil from ships   garbage   _____

                                         (your idea)

Some causes of land pollution:

aluminum   plastic   chemicals   _____
cans   cups   *(your idea)*

6-D What are the causes of pollution? Fill in the blanks with words from above or your own ideas.

1. *Cars and trucks* _____ pollute the air.

2. _____ pollute the water.

3. _____ pollute the land.

SENTENCE POWER: Using the imperative for instructions and suggestions

6-E   Besides polluting, we are wasting energy and other resources. Teach this child not to pollute or waste. What instructions can you give him? Draw a line to match the beginning and end of each sentence.

1. Turn off — long showers.
2. Don't take — garbage into rivers.
3. Recycle — the lights when you leave a room.
4. Don't throw — products in spray cans.
5. Take — your cans and bottles.
6. Don't buy — a bus instead of a private car.

6-F   Now rewrite the suggestions. Add two of your own.

SAVE THE PLANET!

1. *Turn off the lights when you leave a room.*

2.

3.

4.

5.

6.

7.

8.

6-G   **INDEPENDENT GRAMMAR STUDY: The Imperative**
Turn to page 108 in the Grammar Appendix.

STOP AND THINK: Providing specific examples

 6-H   Here are four environmental problems. Talk with a partner and try to find some examples of each problem from anywhere in the world.

1. Cities with bad air pollution: _Los Angeles_

2. Polluted rivers or lakes: _Mississippi River_

3. Polluted oceans or seas: _Mediterranean Sea_

4. Damaged forests: _in Washington State_

Write your examples on the board. Locate the places on a world map if you can.

TALK IT OVER: Saving the planet

6-I   Form a group of three or four. Imagine you are a team of environmental experts. Read about the three problems below. Your group will have the time and money to work on only *one* problem in the next five years. Which one is the most serious? Which one will your group try to solve?

See the Helpful Language on the next page before you begin your discussion.

Pollution in the North Sea

The North Sea, which separates Britain from Holland and Denmark, is polluted with chemicals, oil from ships, and garbage. Seals are dying, and the fishing industry is in trouble.

Switzerland
Ancient Forests Are Damaged

Over 50 percent of the forests in Switzerland have been damaged by acid rain, air pollution, and development. Animals are disappearing. In the future, children may not be able to enjoy these beautiful forests.

Smog in Beijing, China

The city of Beijing (population 6 million) burns coal for energy and heat. The smoke causes one of the worst air pollution problems in the world. People become sick from the smoke, and many die young.

Our team of experts will work on the problem in

BEIJING   SWITZERLAND   THE NORTH SEA. (Circle one.)

HELPFUL LANGUAGE

DESCRIBING THE PROBLEMS

In _____, { people / trees / seals and fish } are dying. / are in danger. { The smog / The acid rain / The pollution } is terrible.

EXPRESSING AN OPINION

We should try to solve the problem in (Beijing).
The (tree) problem in (Switzerland) is the most urgent.

EXPRESSING A DIFFERENT OPINION

I think { old trees / the fishing industry / people's health } is/are more important.

6-J   With your group, complete these sentences.

In our opinion, the most urgent problem is _____

_____ . We want to work on

this problem first because _____

_____ .

6-K   Be ready to write your sentences on the board and/or to explain your decision to the rest of the class. Do the other groups agree with you?

WRITING REVIEW: An expository paragraph

6-L   Use your own ideas to complete these sentences.

Our planet is beautiful, but it is in danger. The environmental

problem that worries me most is _____

_____

_____

because _____

_____

_____.

It is a _____ problem.

To solve it, I think we should _____

_____

_____

_____.

If nothing is done soon, _____

_____

_____.

Family Ties

7 **PLAY MATCHMAKER**
You and your classmates work for a dating service. Your job is to match Gladys, a young fashion designer, with one of three eligible men.

8 **DIVIDE THE HOUSEHOLD CHORES**
You are members of a very busy family. Now you must decide how to divide the household chores in a fair way.

*9 **HELP OUT WITH FAMILY PROBLEMS**
You work for the Family Social Services Department in your town. Which "help line" telephone services should your town have in languages other than English?

*more challenging

HELPFUL LANGUAGE REFERENCE

The following expressions may be helpful in your discussions. Refer to them as needed.

AGREEING	DISAGREEING
Yes, I think you're right.	*I don't agree.*
I agree.	*I disagree.*
That's a good point.	*I don't think so.*

GIVING FEEDBACK (showing you are listening)
I see your point.
OK.
Right.
Uh-huh.

ASKING FOR CLARIFICATION
What do you mean?
What did you say?
Could you explain that?

BRINGING SOMEONE INTO THE CONVERSATION
*What do **you** think about this?*
*What's **your** opinion?*
Do you agree (with me, with John)?

MAKING A NEW SUGGESTION
Let's talk about _____.
Let's think about _____.
How about _____?
What about _____?

COMING TO A CONSENSUS
Does everybody agree?
Let's decide.
We have to decide now.
What's our final decision?

7 Play Matchmaker

WARMING UP: Looking at personal qualities

7-A Which words describe these people? Match the adjectives with the pictures. (Some adjectives fit more than one picture.)

hardworking	funny	intelligent	well-dressed
strong	romantic	good-looking	rich
sensitive	cheerful	talkative	

7-B Which two qualities are the most important in a partner or spouse*? Tell a partner.

(I think) she/he should be (sensitive).

*husband or wife

WORD POWER: Words to describe people

7-C   Find pairs of opposites in the box and write them below. Check your answers on page 129 in the Answer Appendix.

TALKATIVE   rich   POOR   serious

STRONG   hardworking

FUNNY   weak   insensitive

unromantic   lazy   romantic

quiet   sad   cheerful   sensitive

____rich____ / ___poor___   _____ / _____

_____ / _____   _____ / _____

_____ / _____   _____ / _____

_____ / _____   _____ / _____

SENTENCE POWER: Using *both of/neither of* to compare two people

7-D   Which of the above words describe you? Discuss your qualities with a partner. Then write sentences comparing the two of you.

Examples: *I'm quiet, but Sue is talkative.* (difference)
I'm serious, and Sue is too. ⎫
Both of us are serious. ⎭ (similarity)

1. _____

2. _____

3. _____

4. _____

7-E INDEPENDENT GRAMMAR STUDY: *Both of* and *Neither of*
Turn to page 109 in the Grammar Appendix.

STOP AND THINK: Thinking about good partners

7-F In your opinion, which qualities are important in a partner or spouse? Rank these in order of importance from 1 to 8. (1 = most important, 2 = second most important, and so on.)

_____	to be funny	_____	to be rich
_____	to be good-looking	_____	to be romantic
_____	to be intelligent	_____	to be sensitive
_____	to be hardworking	_____	to be cheerful

Show your ranking to a partner. Do you both agree about the most important quality in a partner or spouse? Tell the class your opinion.

The most important thing is to be (rich)!

7-G Is it better to be **similar to** or **very different from** your partner? Discuss this with the class.

Think of a happy couple you know. Do the partners have the same interests or very different ones? Compare them.

Example: *Ana loves to dance, and Sergio does too.*
Ana likes to read, but Sergio doesn't.

1. _____

2. _____

3. _____

4. _____

TALK IT OVER: Playing matchmaker

7-H   Form a group of three or four. You all work for a dating service that tries to match single people with suitable partners. Gladys, below, is a client. Choose a match for her. You have three possible partners (Troy, Peter, and Carlos on page 45).

HELPFUL LANGUAGE

DESCRIBING SOMEONE
Carlos is unromantic and talkative.
Peter is young. He's an actor.
Troy is hardworking.

MAKING COMPARISONS
Gladys is twenty-five, and Troy is too.
Both of them like karate.
Neither of them is lazy.
Gladys likes to swim, but Peter doesn't.
Gladys is romantic, but Carlos isn't.

EXPRESSING AN OPINION
In my opinion, Gladys should date _____.
I think Gladys should date _____.

Gladys

AGE:	25
JOB:	fashion designer
SALARY:	$25,000
HOBBIES:	going to movies, reading
SPORTS:	swimming and karate
PERSONALITY:	romantic, serious, hardworking
BIGGEST WEAKNESS:	sometimes too serious

Troy

AGE:	27
JOB:	police officer
SALARY:	$24,000
HOBBIES:	photography
SPORTS:	karate, skiing
PERSONALITY:	hardworking, quiet, cheerful
BIGGEST WEAKNESS:	sometimes insensitive to other people

Peter

AGE:	23
JOB:	actor
SALARY:	$18,000
HOBBIES:	cooking, going to movies
SPORTS:	soccer, baseball
PERSONALITY:	romantic, sensitive
BIGGEST WEAKNESS:	sometimes lazy

Carlos

AGE:	36
JOB:	businessman
SALARY:	$55,000
HOBBIES:	chess
SPORTS:	none
PERSONALITY:	unromantic, funny, hardworking
BIGGEST WEAKNESS:	sometimes talks too much

7-I   With your group, complete this sentence.

We matched Gladys with _____ because

_____

_____

_____.

7-J   Compare your decision with those of other groups.
Do you all agree?

READING AND WRITING REVIEW: A questionnaire

7-K   Fill in this questionnaire about your "ideal" partner. Check (√) the appropriate boxes.

I think an ideal partner should	IMPORTANT	SOMEWHAT IMPORTANT	UNIMPORTANT
be someone my family likes.			
be very similar to me.			
have the same native language as I do.			
have the same religion as I do.			
like to cook.			
like to read.			
like to dance.			
like children.			
like sports.			
like music.			
be well educated.			
be funny.			
be kind.			
be hardworking.			
be romantic.			
be rich.			
be good-looking.			
(other) _____			

Share your ideas with the class. Your instructor may ask you to write a paragraph about what is important to you in a partner.

8 Divide the Household Chores

WARMING UP: Looking at household chores

8-A Managing a household is a lot of work. What household chores are these people doing? Match the words or phrases with the pictures.

cooking dinner
doing dishes
shopping for groceries
washing the car

walking the dog
taking out the garbage
mopping the floor

vacuuming
dusting
doing the laundry

 8-B **INDEPENDENT GRAMMAR STUDY: Present Continuous**
Turn to page 110 in the Grammar Appendix.

WORD POWER: Names of more household chores

8–C   Circle each word or phrase that describes a household chore. Check your answers on page 130 in the Answer Appendix.

SENTENCE POWER: Using *like, not mind,* and *hate* to express likes and dislikes.

8-D   Read how Vlado feels about these chores.

Now consider each chore below. Talk with a partner. Does your partner like it? not mind it? hate it? Listen and circle the face that shows your partner's feelings.

HOW _____ **FEELS ABOUT THESE CHORES**
(Write your partner's name.)

Cooking dinner

Cleaning the bathroom

Washing the dishes

Dusting

Vacuuming the rug

Shopping for groceries

Doing the laundry

Taking out the garbage

Changing a light bulb

Making the bed

Be ready to report to the class about your partner.

Masako likes _____, and she doesn't mind _____, but she hates _____.

STOP AND THINK: Considering traditional roles

8-E   Who usually did each of these chores in your family when you were growing up? Check (√) the appropriate boxes.

	Mother	*Father*	*You*	*Sister*	*Brother*	*Other**
cooked dinner						
washed the dishes						
shopped for groceries						
took out the garbage						
washed the car						
watched the younger children						
made the beds						
set the table						
repaired the sink						
did the laundry						

*a grandparent, a maid, or anyone else

8-F   **INDEPENDENT GRAMMAR STUDY: Simple Past and Adverbs of Frequency**
Turn to page 112 in the Grammar Appendix.

8-G   With a partner, talk about the chores in 8–E. Who did the chores in your partner's family?

> Partner 1:   **66 Who cooked in your family? 99**
>
> Partner 2:   **66 My mother *always* cooked dinner. But my brother *usually* helped. 99**

Now write three sentences comparing your families when you were growing up.

Examples: *Ming's father often washed the dishes, and my father did too.*
Ming cooked dinner, but I never did.

1. _____

   _____

2. _____

   _____

3. _____

   _____

TALK IT OVER: Dividing household chores

8-H   Form a group of three or four. You are a family. Choose one of these roles: **Mother (M), Father (F), Teenage Son (S),** or **Teenage Daughter (D).**

Mother and Father work full-time, and the children go to school and study during the week. Chores must be done evenings and on Saturdays. Who will do what? Discuss the chores with your family and fill in the boxes below with the initials (M, F, S, and D).

See the HELPFUL LANGUAGE on the next page before beginning your discussion.

		Sunday	Monday	Tuesday	Wednesday	Thursday	Friday	Saturday
cook dinner	(60 minutes)							
wash the dishes	(30)							
dust	(30)	■		■		■		■
take out the garbage	(10)							
vacuum	(30)	■		■		■		■
wash the car	(60)	■	■	■	■	■	■	
mop the floors	(30)	■	■	■	■	■	■	
walk the dog	(15)							
shop for groceries	(45)	■		■		■		■

Now add up the total work time for each family member. Is your schedule fair?

Mother: _____ hours

Father: _____ hours

Son: _____ hours

Daughter: _____ hours

HELPFUL LANGUAGE

OFFERING TO DO SOMETHING AND GIVING REASONS

I'll cook on Mondays.   *I don't mind cooking.*

I can cook on Tuesdays and Thursdays.   *It's fun/easy/not bad.*

REFUSING TO DO SOMETHING AND GIVING REASONS

I'd rather not cook.   *It's not fun.*

I can't cook. I don't know how. *It's boring.*

I hate vacuuming.   *It takes too long.*

ASKING SOMEONE TO DO SOMETHING

Will you wash the dishes?

Why don't you wash the dishes?

You should do your share. How about it?

8–I   Share some of your group's ideas with the class. Should each family member work the same number of hours in the home?

WRITING REVIEW: A list of things to do

8–J   What chores do you have to do this week? Make a list. Use the imperative form.

Do the laundry.

Help Out with Family Problems

WARMING UP: Looking at difficult family situations

9–A   Nowadays family life can be difficult. The pictures on this page show some of the situations that modern families face. Match the pictures with the following words or phrases.

physical violence or abuse
alcohol or drug abuse
unemployment or
   problems on the job

difficulties with school
balancing home and jobs
disagreements between
   parents and children

divorce
health problems
financial problems

9–B   Can you think of another kind of difficult family situation? Which situations are the most serious, in your opinion? Which ones are the most common?

WORD POWER: Names of organizations and services that can help

9–C   In the United States, there are many agencies and telephone services to help people with problems. With your instructor, decide who these people can call for help.

1. An eighteen-year-old boy is drinking regularly.

   _____

2. A woman in her forties is tired all the time.

   _____

3. A sixteen-year-old girl wants to leave school.

   _____

4. A married couple argues and fights a lot.

   _____

5. A man in his thirties takes sleeping pills every night.

   _____

6. A ten-year-old child is often hit by his parents.

   _____

> Alcoholics Anonymous[1]
>
> Child Abuse Hot Line[2]
>
> Marriage Counseling
>
> The Police
>
> Planned Parenthood[3]
>
> Teen Counseling
>
> Drug Abuse Hot Line
>
> Health Help Line
>
> City Job Services
>
> A Religious Leader

1. Alcoholics Anonymous (AA) is an organization that helps members with their drinking problems.

2. A Child Abuse Hot Line is a telephone service that gives advice to callers about the bad treatment of children.

3. Planned Parenthood is a service that gives information and help to people interested in birth control.

9–D   Work with a partner. Look at what Ramon is thinking and discuss these questions: Is Ramon right? Why or why not?

Be ready to share your ideas with the class.

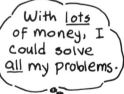

With **lots** of money, I could solve **all** my problems.

SENTENCE POWER: Using *should* and *shouldn't* to give advice

9-E   **INDEPENDENT GRAMMAR STUDY:** *Should/Shouldn't*
Turn to page 114 in the Grammar Appendix.

9-F   Role-play with a partner. You are two friends. One of you is talking about a situation in your family. The other gives advice with *should* or *shouldn't*. Then change roles. Follow the model. Add your own ideas if you like!

> Partner 1:   **❝ Luis smokes a pack of cigarettes a day! ❞**
>
> Partner 2:   **❝ He should stop smoking. He shouldn't smoke. ❞**

Situation	Advice
Luis smokes a pack of cigarettes a day.	_____ stop smoking. _____ not smoke.
My cousin Sue needs a job.	_____ call City Job Services. _____ read the "Help Wanted" ads in the newspaper.
Raul is drinking a lot of beer tonight!	_____ not drive. _____ take a taxi home.
Laura has a very bad cold.	_____ stay in bed. _____ not go to school.
My 15-year-old brother is having trouble at school.	_____ talk to _____. _____ call Teen Counseling.
My mother has frequent headaches.	_____ see a doctor. _____ call the Health Help Line.
I'm having trouble at work with my boss.	_____ talk to _____.

STOP AND THINK: Deciding on the best course of action

9-G   Form a group of three or four. Read about the following situations, and then decide what you should do in each case. (Note: Answers are not "right" or "wrong.")

1. You saw your neighbor hit his five-year-old child. You often see black-and-blue marks on the child's body. What should you do?
    a. Tell the neighbor to stop.
    b. Call the Child Abuse Hot Line.
    c. Call the police.
    d. Do nothing. (Stay out of it.)

    e. Other:_____.

2. Your sister Ruth, age thirty-two, is drinking heavily. Nobody in your family—including Ruth's husband, Eric—is talking about Ruth's drinking, but you think it's a problem. What should you do?
    a. Talk to Ruth.
    b. Talk to Eric.
    c. Call your pastor (priest, minister, rabbi, imam, or other religious leader).
    d. Call Alcoholics Anonymous (AA).

    e. Other: _____.

3. Your cousin Anna is seventeen years old. She lives at home with her parents. She is not married and is expecting a baby. She feels alone and afraid. What should she do?
    a. She should talk to her parents.
    b. She should ask her boyfriend to marry her.
    c. She should call Planned Parenthood or an adoption agency.*
    d. She should drop out of school.

    e. Other: _____.

*an agency that places children with new parents

Share your ideas with the class.

TALK IT OVER: Helping out with family problems

9-H   Form a group of three or four. You are members of the Family Social Services Department in your town. There are now eight help lines available in English. There is money to make *two* of these help lines available in other languages.

See HELPFUL LANGUAGE on the next page before you begin your discussion.

HELP LINES*

ALCOHOLICS ANONYMOUS 555-2337	HEALTH HELP LINE 555-3100
CHILD ABUSE HOT LINE 555-4407	MARRIAGE COUNSELING 555-8228
CITY JOB SERVICES 555-0557	PLANNED PARENTHOOD 555-4772
DRUG ABUSE HOT LINE 555-6037	TEEN COUNSELING 555-9109

*These are not real numbers. (You can get the numbers for your area by dialing Directory Assistance.)

We should have the following two help lines in additional languages:

1. [   ]

2. [   ]

9–1 With your group, complete these sentences.

We chose 1 because _____

_____

_____ .

We chose 2 because _____

_____

_____ .

Be ready to share your ideas with the class.

HELPFUL LANGUAGE

MAKING SUGGESTIONS/PROPOSING IDEAS
Drugs are a big problem in this community.
I think the Marriage Counseling Help Line is a good idea.
Let's choose the City Job Services Help Line.

GIVING REASONS
Many people have questions about drug problems.
Lots of married couples need to talk to a counselor.
Many people need jobs, and City Job Services can help.

COMMENTING ON OTHER PEOPLE'S IDEAS
That's a good point.
Yes, I agree.
No, I don't think so.
Hmmm. But what about the Child Abuse Hot Line?

WRITING REVIEW: A list of suggestions

9-J   This young family wants to have a happy and healthy family life.

In the space below, list three more things that they *should* or *shouldn't* do to have a good life.

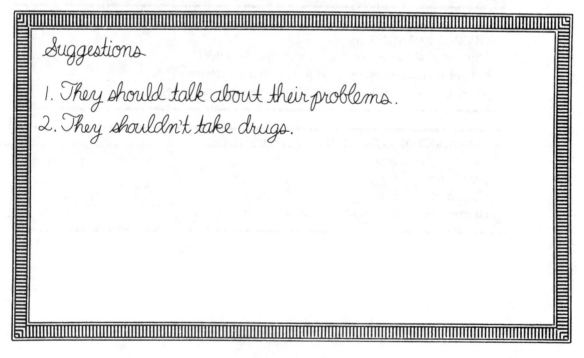

Suggestions

1. They should talk about their problems.
2. They shouldn't take drugs.

Shopping and Other Money Matters

10 GIVE A GIFT
You have only $50 to buy gifts for three special people.
What will you choose?

11 WORK OUT A FAMILY BUDGET
Your family keeps running out of money each month.
Now you have to sit down and decide what your
financial priorities are.

*12 DECIDE ON APPROPRIATE SALARIES
You are the owners of a new health food cafeteria. You
are going to hire seven employees, and now you need
to decide what their salaries will be.

*more challenging

HELPFUL LANGUAGE REFERENCE

The following expressions may be helpful in your discussions. Refer to them as needed.

AGREEING	**DISAGREEING**
Yes, I think you're right.	*I don't agree.*
I agree.	*I disagree.*
That's a good point.	*I don't think so.*

GIVING FEEDBACK (showing you are listening)
I see your point.
OK.
Right.
Uh-huh.

ASKING FOR CLARIFICATION
What do you mean?
What did you say?
Could you explain that?

BRINGING SOMEONE INTO THE CONVERSATION
*What do **you** think about this?*
*What's **your** opinion?*
Do you agree (with me, with John)?

MAKING A NEW SUGGESTION
Let's talk about _____ .
Let's think about _____ .
How about _____ ?
What about _____ ?

COMING TO A CONSENSUS
Does everybody agree?
Let's decide.
We have to decide now.
What's our final decision?

10 Give a Gift

WARMING UP: Looking at items in a catalog

10–A Look at these items from a store catalog. Match the items with their names below.

towels   sweatshirt   cap   box of
cologne   hair dryer   teddy bear   chocolates
necklace   watches   sunglasses   atlas
                                        tie

a. $20.00
b. $22.00
c. $17.00
d. $12.00
e. $25.00
f. $10.00
g. $10.00
h. $18.00
i. $15.00
j. $9.95
k. $11.00 each
l. $13.00

10–B Talk to a partner. Which catalog items do you have? Which would you like to get as a gift?

I have (a watch), but I'd like to get (an atlas).

63

WORD POWER: Words to describe things

10-C   Circle the best adjective for the gift in each picture. Use the definitions below if you need to.

1. unusual
    (cute)
    elegant

2. wild
    cute
    delicious

3. useful
    pretty
    wild

4. good-looking
    delicious
    funny

5. interesting
    pretty
    expensive
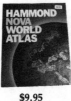
$9.95

6. stylish
    cute
    cheap

$18.00

---

cheap   low in price; inexpensive: *Fresh fruit is cheap in Mexico.*

cute   attractive, and often small: *What a cute child!*

delicious   having a good taste or smell: *Lunch was delicious.*

elegant   pleasing to the eye; in good taste: *Jacqueline Kennedy Onassis wears elegant clothes.*

expensive   costing a lot of money: *Houses, cars, and boats are expensive items.*—opposite of **inexpensive**

funny   1. amusing; causing laughter: *It's a funny story.* 2. Unusual; strange: *What's that funny noise?*

good-looking   nice to look at: *That's a good-looking suit.*

interesting   attracting attention; unusual: *What interesting ideas you have!*—opposite of **boring**

pretty   lovely; good-looking: *Those are pretty flowers.*

stylish   being in fashion: *What a stylish hat!*

unusual   not common; different: *He has unusual handwriting.*

useful   helpful: *Dictionaries are useful.*

wild   crazy; excessive; not usual: *She wears wild clothes.*

SENTENCE POWER: Using *but*

10-D Role-play with a partner. One of you is a fussy* customer in Lucy's Gift Shop. The other is Lucy. The customer has won a gift certificate from the shop and wants to choose something. Lucy is making suggestions to the customer.

*not easily satisfied

Use adjectives from 10–C to talk about the items below.

Partner 1 (Lucy):	66 **How about this cap?** 99
Partner 2 (Customer):	66 **It's very cute, *but* it's not my style.** 99
	66 **It's elegant, *but* expensive.** 99

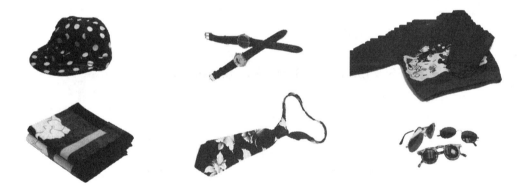

STOP AND THINK: Deciding on good gifts

10-E   Work with a partner. Choose birthday gifts from the catalog on page 63 for these people. Write your reasons.

1. Jorge, a 28-year-old soccer player

   GIFT: _____

   REASON: _____

2. Nina, an active 85-year-old woman

   GIFT: _____

   REASON: _____

3. Jemal, your bright 6-year-old nephew

   GIFT: _____

   REASON: _____

4. Sevil, a busy 48-year-old businesswoman

   GIFT: _____

   REASON: _____

5. Bogdan, a newly married 19-year-old man

   GIFT: _____

   REASON: _____

10-F   Share your gift ideas with the rest of the class. Make sentences with *because* or *so*. Follow this model.

> *We'll give Jorge towels **because** he takes lots of showers.*
> *Jorge takes lots of showers, **so** we'll give him towels.*

Do others in the class agree with your choices?

10-G   **INDEPENDENT GRAMMAR STUDY:** *Because* and *So*
Turn to page 115 in the Grammar Appendix.

TALK IT OVER: Giving a gift

10-G Form a group of three or four. Suppose you are all brothers and sisters. You have $50. You must buy gifts from the catalog for these three people.

- Your sick grandfather.
  He is ninety years old and spends most of the day in bed.

- Your neighbor Paula. Her thirteenth birthday will be next week.

- Your rich, sophisticated cousin Mark, age 18.
  He is graduating from high school this month.

HELPFUL LANGUAGE

MAKING A SUGGESTION
How about (a box of chocolates) for Grandpa?*
Let's get (a box of chocolates) for Grandpa.
He would like (the box of chocolates).

AGREEING
Good idea. It's perfect for him.
Yes, it looks delicious.
Yes, he'd love it.

DISAGREEING
No, it's too expensive/cheap.
No, Grandpa is sick.
No, I prefer to buy him (an atlas).

*a common short form for *grandfather*

Write your choices here.   *PRICES*

For Grandfather: _____ _____

For Paula: _____ _____

For Cousin Mark: _____ _____

                              TOTAL: _____ (Must be $50 or less!)

10-H   With your group, complete these sentences.

1. We chose* the _____ for Grandfather

   because _____

   _____.

2. We chose the _____ for Paula

   because _____

   _____.

3. We chose the _____ for Cousin Mark

   because _____

   _____.

Chose is the past form of *choose*.

10-J   Explain your group's choices to the class. Do the other groups agree with you?

WRITING REVIEW: Personal thank-you notes

10-K   Rewrite these thank-you notes from Grandfather, Paula, and Mark. Supply the missing words and choose the appropriate forms.

Oct. 15

Dear Neighbors,
I love the _____ that
_____ you gave me.
It's/They're _____
and just perfect for
me. I'm sure I'll
enjoy it/them!

Love,
Paula

October 12
Dearest Grandchildren,
Thank you so much for
_____ !
It's/They're _____
I'm feeling much
better. Come and
see me soon !

Your Grandpa

October 11
Dear Cousins,
It was so nice of you to
send the_____ for my
graduation. _____
_____
_____.

Yours,   Mark

11 Work Out a Family Budget

WARMING UP: Looking at the cost of everyday activities

11–A Which of these sayings do you agree with? Why?

Money makes the world go round.
The best things in life are free.

Look at the activities below. Circle the *free* ones.

11–B Find these activities in the pictures: singing, dancing, reading the newspaper, hugging, playing volleyball, laughing, watching TV, going to the movies, going to school, eating out, getting a haircut, reading a book.

Now discuss the cost of each activity with the class.

Examples: *Singing is free.*
Reading a newspaper is inexpensive.
Eating out is expensive.

11-C   **INDEPENDENT GRAMMAR STUDY: Gerunds as Subjects**
Turn to page 116 in the Grammar Appendix.

WORD POWER: Words for everyday purchases and expenses

11-D   Which of these items have you paid for recently?

Put a check (√) in front of each item you have paid for recently. Write the
amount you paid.

		COST			COST	
__	shoes	_____	__	light bulb	_____	
__	eggs	_____	__	phone	_____	
__	aspirin	_____	__	phone bill	_____	
__	T-shirt	_____	__	hamburger	_____	
__	onions	_____	__	toothpaste	_____	
__	magazine	_____	__	gas	_____	per gallon/liter

11-E   Talk with a partner. Compare what you bought this week, how
much you paid for each item, and where you bought each item. Follow the
model.

> Partner 1:   " **Did you buy a hamburger this week?** "
>
> Partner 2:   " **Yes. I paid $1.50 for a burger at Burger Boy.** "

STOP AND THINK: Categorizing your monthly expenses

11–F   What are some things you have paid for in the past month? Put the items in the correct categories.

HOUSING AND UTILITIES	*FOOD*	*CLOTHES*	*TRANSPORTATION*

ENTERTAINMENT AND RECREATION	*EDUCATION*	*PERSONAL ITEMS*	*HEALTH/MEDICAL CARE*

11–G   For you, which category is your *biggest* expense every month? Which category is your *smallest* expense? Discuss this with the class.

TALK IT OVER: Working out a family budget

11-H   Form a group of three or four. You are a family. Take one of these roles: **Mother**; **Father**; sixteen-year-old daughter, **Nancy**; fourteen-year-old son, **Jack**.

Mother and Father work full-time. Nancy and Jack go to school and work part-time. Your family keeps running out of* money. You decide to sit down together and work out a family budget. After paying housing and utilities and education costs each month, your family has $1,000 left. How will you spend it? Fill out the monthly budget form below.

*using up or finishing something

HELPFUL LANGUAGE

EXPRESSING OPINIONS AND DISAGREEING ABOUT BUDGETS
Let's spend lots of money on (clothes).
No. (Buying good food) is more important.

We need some money for (movies).
No. (Going to movies) is too expensive.
Let's watch TV.

MORE ABOUT BUDGETS
How much do we need for _____ ?
We need more money for _____ .
Let's spend less money on _____ .
How much should we save?
     _____ is/are expensive.
     _____ is/are inexpensive.

MONTHLY BUDGET	
TOTAL INCOME	**$1,600**
HOUSING AND UTILITIES	500
EDUCATION	100
FOOD	
CLOTHES	
TRANSPORTATION	
ENTERTAINMENT AND RECREATION	
MEDICINES*	
PERSONAL ITEMS	
SAVINGS	
(OTHER)	
TOTAL EXPENSES:	

*Other health/medical costs are paid by parents' insurance.

11-I   Be ready to write your budget on the board and explain your reasons to the class.

WRITING REVIEW: A personal budget

11-J   Choose either option A or option B.

OPTION A: Write about your spending habits. Fill in the blanks below.

I spend a lot of money on _____ ,
                              (What?)

usually about _____ a month. This
                    (How much?)

is because _____ .
              (Why?)

I also like to spend money on _____ .
                                  (What else?)

For instance, I recently bought _____
                                    (What specific item?)

at _____ for _____ .
      (What store?)   (How much?)

In general, I feel _____ about/with my
                        (How?)

spending habits.

OPTION B: Make a budget for yourself—either for next week, next month, or next year. Write your expenses in order of importance. Eliminate the least important expenses if you don't have enough money.

March Budget

Income	$950
Housing and utilities	$365
Food	$280 ($70/week)
Transportation	$44 ($2 × 22 wks)
Clothes	$75 (jeans and sweater)
Entertainment	

Decide on Appropriate Salaries

12

WARMING UP: Looking at jobs

12-A Would you like a job at a health food cafeteria? Sunrise Cafeteria has just opened and needs to hire seven people for the following positions. Match the names of the jobs with the pictures.

busboy

business manager

cashier

chef

custodian

dishwasher

guitarist

12-B In your opinion, which job is the most interesting? the most boring? the easiest? the most difficult?

74

WORD POWER: Work verbs

12–C   Work with a partner. What work do these employees do? Fill in the blanks with phrases from the box below, or write your own ideas.

1. A cashier *takes money*
   and *gives customers a receipt* .

2. A guitarist _____
   and _____ .

3. A chef _____
   and _____ .

4. A dishwasher _____
   and _____ .

5. A business manager _____
   and _____ .

6. A custodian _____
   and _____ .

7. A busboy _____
   and _____ .

entertains people	chops vegetables
clears the tables	pays the bills
cooks large meals	cleans the rest rooms
mops the floor	washes the dishes
scrubs pots and pans	orders supplies and equipment
takes money	plays the guitar
supervises employees	gives customers a receipt
washes windows	washes the tables

SENTENCE POWER: Using *can* and *have to* to express possibility and necessity

12-D   Talk with a partner about the different jobs at the cafeteria. How do you feel about these jobs? Study the sample conversation. Use words and phrases from the boxes if you wish.

Partner 1:	66 **Cashiers have an easy job.** 99
Partner 2:	66 **Why do you think so?** 99
Partner 1:	66 **They can sit down all day.** 99

NOTE: Use *can* to express possibility.
          Use *have to* to express obligation or necessity.

Busboys Business managers Cashiers Chefs Custodians Dishwashers Guitarists	have a/an	interesting boring easy hard/tough rewarding awful	job.

They can/have to

talk to a lot of people
work fast.
relax as they work.
meet new people.
sit down all day.
do hard physical work.
move a lot.
stand up all day.
think a lot.
supervise employees.
worry about money.
be creative.
(your idea).

12-E   **INDEPENDENT GRAMMAR STUDY:** *Have to/Has to* **and** *Can*
Turn to page 117 in the Grammar Appendix.

STOP AND THINK: Evaluating your work preferences

12-F   Which of these jobs are interesting to you? Rank them in order of interest from 1 to 7. (1 = most interesting, 2 = second most interesting, and so on.)

_____	busboy	_____	custodian
_____	business manager	_____	dishwasher
_____	cashier	_____	guitarist
_____	chef		

12-G   What are you looking for in a job? Fill out this questionnaire. Put a check (√) under YES, MAYBE, or NO.

I want a job where I can—	Yes, very important	Maybe important	No, not important
sit down.			
move around a lot.			
work outside.			
sit at a desk.			
meet many new people.			
work for myself/be independent.			
earn a good salary.			
have weekends and evenings free.			
be creative.			
travel.			
do a variety of things.			
relax.			
be useful to society.			
make decisions.			
work with a computer.			
learn new things.			

Share your work preferences with the class.

TALK IT OVER: Deciding on appropriate salaries

12-H   Form a group of three or four. You are co-owners of the new health food cafeteria, Sunrise Cafeteria. You must decide on the salaries for your seven new positions: **busboy, business manager, cashier, chef, custodian, dishwasher,** and **guitarist**. Every employee will work full-time, forty hours a week. Your total budget for salaries is $160,000 a year. You cannot spend more than this.

HELPFUL LANGUAGE

GIVING OPINIONS ABOUT JOBS
A dishwasher has a difficult job.
She/he has to work fast and stand up all day.

DISAGREEING
No, it's easy! Dishwashers don't have to think a lot.

GIVING OPINIONS ABOUT SALARIES
She should get a big/small salary.
He should make twenty thousand dollars ($20,000).

DISAGREEING
That's too much!
That's too little!

JOB	*YEARLY SALARY*
Busboy	_____
Business manager	_____
Cashier	_____
Chef	_____
Custodian	_____
Dishwasher	_____
Guitarist	_____
TOTAL:	_____

12-I With your group, complete these sentences.

The _____ should get the highest salary,

_____, because _____

_____ .

The _____ should get the lowest salary,

_____, because _____

_____ .

12-J Discuss your decisions with the class.

WRITING REVIEW: Employment confirmation letters

12-K As an owner of Sunrise Cafeteria, you are sending out letters to your new employees. You have written a letter to the custodian. Now write to one of the other employees.

Sunrise Cafeteria

TO: New employee
RE: Job description and salary
DATE: Feb. 27 _____, 1992

Welcome to Sunrise Cafeteria. This is to confirm your position with our company.
Job: Custodian _____
Yearly salary: $21,000 _____

Your responsibilities include the following:

1. mop the floors daily _____

2. wash the windows weekly _____

3. clean the restrooms _____

4. take out the garbage _____

We look forward to working with you.

Sunrise Cafeteria

TO: New employee
RE: Job description and salary
DATE: _____, 199__

Welcome to Sunrise Cafeteria. This is to confirm your position with our company.
Job: _____
Yearly salary: _____

Your responsibilities include the following:

1. _____

2. _____

3. _____

4. _____

We look forward to working with you.

Going Places

HELPFUL LANGUAGE REFERENCE

The following expressions may be helpful in your discussions. Refer to them as needed.

AGREEING	DISAGREEING
Yes, I think you're right.	*I don't agree.*
I agree.	*I disagree.*
That's a good point.	*I don't think so.*

GIVING FEEDBACK (showing you are listening)
I see your point.
OK.
Right.
Uh-huh.

ASKING FOR CLARIFICATION
What do you mean?
What did you say?
Could you explain that?

BRINGING SOMEONE INTO THE CONVERSATION
*What do **you** think about this?*
*What's **your** opinion?*
Do you agree (with me, with John)?

MAKING A NEW SUGGESTION
Let's talk about _____.
Let's think about _____.
How about _____?
What about _____?

COMING TO A CONSENSUS
Does everybody agree?
Let's decide.
We have to decide now.
What's our final decision?

13 Pick Your Perfect Vacation

WARMING UP: Looking over vacation ads

13-A Look at these ads for package vacations. Circle new words. Can you guess their meanings?

WILD WEST VACATION OF YOUR DREAMS!

Spend 2 weeks on a ranch in Montana!

Live like a cowboy. Ride a horse through beautiful, quiet mountain scenery.

Simple accommodations. Home cooking.

Average May temp. 14° C/ 57° F.

PUERTO RICO
The Shining Star of The Caribbean

14 glorious days in paradise!

Luxury hotel on a beautiful beach. Swimming, sailing, fine food, discos.

Average May temp. 27° C/ 80° F.

EGYPT

Exciting 10-day cruise on the Nile River!

See the Great Sphinx and climb the 2,000-year-old Giza pyramids.

Average May temp. 25° C/ 77° F.

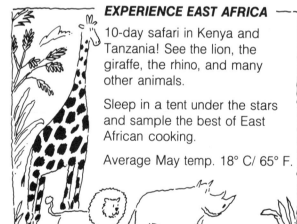

EXPERIENCE EAST AFRICA

10-day safari in Kenya and Tanzania! See the lion, the giraffe, the rhino, and many other animals.

Sleep in a tent under the stars and sample the best of East African cooking.

Average May temp. 18° C/ 65° F.

13-B Talk to a partner. Which vacations look the most interesting to you? Why?

WORD POWER: Things to do on vacation

13-C   Work with a partner. Write what you can do in the different places. Look at the ads on page 83 or use the phrases below.

sleep in a tent	live in the mountains	sunbathe
climb a pyramid	see historical monuments	swim
live on a ship	taste East African food	relax
eat home cooking	ride horses	sail
see wild animals	eat fine food	dance

1. In Puerto Rico, you can *eat fine food*

    and *swim*   .

    You can also *dance in the evening*   .

2. In Egypt, you can _____

    and _____ .

    You can also _____ .

3. In East Africa, you can _____

    and _____ .

    You can also _____ .

4. In Montana, you can _____

    and _____ .

    You can also _____ .

13-D Interview your partner. What does she or he like to do on vacation?

> Partner 1: **❝ Do you like to see historical monuments? ❞**
>
> Partner 2: **❝ No, I don't. I like to relax on vacation. ❞**

Now write sentences about you and your partner.

1. We both like to _____ on vacation.

2. We don't like to _____ .

STOP AND THINK: Reading between the lines

13-E Look back at the four ads on page 83. These ads show only the good side of each vacation. Do you think there might also be a bad side?

Fill in the blanks with positive and negative words from the box. Give your own opinions.

+ (positive)	− (negative)
fun	boring
exciting	scary
educational	dangerous
relaxing	uncomfortable
beautiful	crowded
quiet	hot
fascinating	

1. The resort in Puerto Rico looks

    exciting and *beautiful*,

    but it might be *crowded* .

2. The cruise on the Nile River looks

    _____ and _____,

    but it might be _____ .

3. The safari in East Africa looks _____ and _____,

    but it might be _____ .

4. The ranch in Montana looks _____ and _____,

    but it might be _____ .

Share your ideas with the class.

SENTENCE POWER: Using common phrases to talk about the weather

13-F   Look back at the ads. What can you say about the weather in May?

In Egypt, *it's warm*_____ .

In Montana, _____ .

In Puerto Rico, _____ .

In East Africa, _____ .

°F	°C	
120	50	very hot
110	40	hot
100	30	
90		warm
80	20	
70		cool
60	10	
50		
40	0	cold
30		
20	10	very cold
10	20	
0	30	

NOTE: If you don't like the weather, you can say,
"The weather is *too* hot." *or* "It's *too* cold."

13-G   **INDEPENDENT GRAMMAR STUDY:** *Too* and *Very*
Turn to page 118 in the Grammar Appendix.

13-H   What is the weather like in your hometown in May? in August? in December? Tell a partner.

It's windy.   It's sunny and cool.   It's rainy.

It's hot and humid.   It's snowy and cold.   It's cloudy.

TALK IT OVER: Picking your perfect vacation

13-I   Form a group of three or four. You are friends. You have just won a trip together to *one* of the places shown on page 83. Together, decide where you will go.

HELPFUL LANGUAGE

EXPRESSING PREFERENCES AND GIVING REASONS
Let's go to _____! It's (relaxing).
_____ is better. You can (swim) there.
I would rather go to _____. The weather there is perfect.

DISAGREEING	**AGREEING**
It's too hot.	*Right.*
It's too cool.	*That's true.*
It's too crowded.	*You've got a point.*
It's too boring.	*I'm with you.*
It isn't fun.	
It isn't relaxing.	
It isn't quiet.	

13-J   With your group, complete these sentences.

We decided to go to _____ because

_____ and

_____ .

Also, _____ .

13-K   Discuss your group's choice with the class. Is your choice a popular one with the class?

WRITING REVIEW: An advertisement

13-L   You work for an ad agency. Write an ad for a two-week package vacation to Paris *or* for a trip to a city in your native country. If you choose the second option, use your own paper and find your own pictures.

Design an ad that attracts many readers!

14 Design In-Flight Uniforms

14-A   When you travel, what kind of clothes do you like to wear? In this lesson, you are going to design work uniforms for people who travel all the time—flight attendants.* But first, find these clothes below.

2 blouses	3 jackets	2 button-down shirts
4 pairs of pants	1 vest	
1 tie; 1 bowtie	1 polo shirt	4 skirts
1 turtleneck top	1 pair of blue jeans	1 sweater

*people who serve you on an airplane

14-B   Talk with a partner about your favorite clothes. What do you like to wear to school? to parties? to work?

WORD POWER: Words to describe clothes

14-C   Below are some adjectives that will help you describe the patterns and colors of clothes. What do you see in 14–A that is *striped, printed, polka dotted,* and so on? Write sentences with *There is (There's)* or *There are.*

NOTE: *Pants* and *blue jeans* are plural nouns.

1. striped

There's a striped jacket _____.
There are striped pants _____.
_____.

2. printed

_____.
_____.

3. polka dotted

_____.
_____.

4. checked

_____.

5. black

_____.
_____.

6. white

_____.
_____.

7. aqua

_____.

 14-D   INDEPENDENT GRAMMAR STUDY: **Order of Adjectives**
Turn to page 119 in the Grammar Appendix.

SENTENCE POWER: Using adjectives to express your opinion on styles

14-E   Discuss these styles with your partner. Give your opinions on the clothes, using some of the adjectives in the box.

> Partner 1:   **66   Do you like the black skirt?   99**
>
> Partner 2:   **66   No. It's* too long and old-fashioned for my taste.   99**

*Use *They're* when talking about pants.

ADJECTIVES

+

pretty

attractive

good-looking

stylish

comfortable

elegant

different

—

ugly

old-fashioned

boring

uncomfortable

too conservative

too wild

too tight

too long

too casual

too dressy

STOP AND THINK: Rating the suitability of clothes

 14-F   Work with a partner. Imagine that you work for a small new airline, FlyRite Air. You are in charge of designing the flight attendants' uniforms. They must be *comfortable* and *attractive*.

How suitable* are these clothes for the flight attendants? Circle your ratings and give reasons if you can. Use the adjectives in 14–E.

*correct or right for the occasion

1.   For Women:

NOT SUITABLE	SOMEWHAT SUITABLE	VERY SUITABLE
0	1	2

For Men:

0	1	2

Reason(s): _____

_____

_____

2.   For Women:

NOT SUITABLE	SOMEWHAT SUITABLE	VERY SUITABLE
0	1	2

For Men:

0	1	2

Reason(s): _____

_____

_____

3.   For Women:

NOT SUITABLE	SOMEWHAT SUITABLE	VERY SUITABLE
0	1	2

For Men:

0	1	2

Reason(s): _____

_____

_____

4.   For Women:

NOT SUITABLE	SOMEWHAT SUITABLE	VERY SUITABLE
0	1	2

For Men:

0	1	2

Reason(s): _____

_____

_____

TALK IT OVER: Designing in-flight uniforms

14–G   Form a group of three or four. You are working together to design the new uniforms for FlyRite's flight attendants. Choose clothes from page 89 or design original ones. Draw the uniforms on the figures below and write descriptions.

NOTE: Many of the clothes on page 89 are unisex; that is, men *or* women can wear them.

HELPFUL LANGUAGE

EXPRESSING OPINIONS AND GIVING REASONS
The men should wear (the print tie). It's (good-looking).
I like (the striped jacket) for women. It's (comfortable).
Men and women should wear the same thing.

EXPRESSING PREFERENCES
I prefer (the tight black pants) for everyone.
I like (the wide black pants) better.

DISAGREEING
But (a tie) is uncomfortable!
But (the striped jacket) is ugly.

Men's uniform: _____

_____

_____

Women's uniform: _____

_____

_____

_____

14-H   Share your group's choices with the class. Explain your reasons. Do other groups agree with you?

WRITING REVIEW: A memo

14-I   Write a memo to Ms. Haddad, the president of your company. Describe your new designs.

FlyRite

TO: Ms. Haddad, President, FlyRite Air

FROM:

RE: New uniforms for flight attendants

DATE:

We have designed the following uniforms for our flight attendants.

The men will wear _____

_____ .

We chose these clothes because _____

_____ .

The women will wear _____

_____ .

We chose this uniform because _____

_____ .

We hope you will approve our designs. Please send us your comments as

soon as possible.

15 Plan a Class Trip

WARMING UP: Looking at places around town

15-A Match these places with their names.

a stadium   an amusement park
an aquarium   a historic monument
a factory   a natural history museum
a zoo   a nature preserve/park

a

b

c

d

e

f

g

h

15-B Which of these places can you find in or near your community? Have you visited any of them? With the class, think of other interesting or fun places to visit in your area. Write your ideas here.

_____   _____

_____   _____

WORD POWER: Things to see and do

15-C   Work with a partner. Use the chart to tell your partner why people visit the different places. Take turns and say as many true sentences as you can.

Example: *People visit an amusement park to ride the roller coaster.*

People visit	an amusement park	to see	trees and plants.
	an aquarium	to learn about	a picnic.
	a factory	to ride	the Ferris wheel.
	a historic monument	to have	the past.
	a natural history museum		a good time.
	a nature preserve		lions and tigers.
	a stadium		other cultures.
	a zoo		how something is made.
			sharks.
			something famous.
			the roller coaster.
			a game.

15-D   Work with a partner. Use the chart to give each other a dictation. One of you will dictate three sentences while the other person covers the chart and writes. Then change roles.

TAKE DICTATION

1. _____

2. _____

3. _____

15-E   INDEPENDENT GRAMMAR STUDY: Infinitives of Purpose
Turn to page 120 in the Grammar Appendix.

STOP AND THINK: Gathering information

15-F Form a group of three or four. You are going to plan a class trip. First, gather your information. Fill in the boxes with things you know about the places in your community. You can write specific names in the parentheses.

If you don't have the information, leave the box empty.

	Where is it?	How far away is it?	How much does it cost to visit?	Is it interesting or fun?
Amusement park				
Aquarium				
Factory ( )				
Monument ( )				
Natural history museum				
Park/preserve ( )				
Stadium				
Zoo				
Other:				
Other:				

15-G Does your group need any additional information? Walk around the room. Ask other students for the information you need. You can ask these questions.

> *Is there (an amusement park) nearby?*
> *Where is it?*
> *How far away is it?*
> *How much does it cost to visit?*
> *Is it interesting or fun?*

You can also ask your instructor or use a phone book to call places for information.

TALK IT OVER: Planning a class trip

15-H   Work with your group from 15–F. Your class will take a class trip. Decide where you will go (one or two places), how you will get there, and how long you will be gone. Fill out the itinerary on the next page.

HELPFUL LANGUAGE

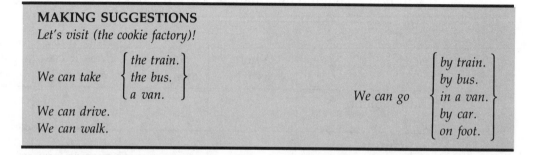

MAKING SUGGESTIONS

Let's visit (the cookie factory)!

We can take { *the train.* / *the bus.* / *a van.* }

We can drive.
We can walk.

We can go { *by train.* / *by bus.* / *in a van.* / *by car.* / *on foot.* }

GIVING REASONS FOR AND AGAINST

It's (not) { *interesting.* / *boring.* / *fun.* / *expensive.* / *far.* / *nearby.* }

ASKING QUESTIONS

Where will we go?
How will we get there?
How long will we stay?
What will we do there?
When will we leave?

PROPOSED ITINERARY FOR CLASS TRIP

Destination #1: _____

Day and time of departure: _____

Means of transportation: _____

Length of stay: _____

Activities: _____

Cost: _____

Destination #2: _____

Day and time of departure: _____

Means of transportation: _____

Length of stay: _____

Activities: _____

Cost: _____

15–I   Share some of your ideas with the class.

15–J   **INDEPENDENT GRAMMAR STUDY: Future with *Will*.**
Turn to page 121 in the Grammar Appendix.

WRITING REVIEW: A memo

15-K   Write a memo to your instructor explaining in detail the trip you have planned.

MEMORANDUM

TO:

FROM (list all group members):

RE:*

DATE:

Our group's proposed itinerary for a class trip looks like this:

We will go to _____ on _____ .
　　　　　　　　　　(Where?)　　　　　　　　　　　　　　　(What day?)

We will leave at _____ and go by/on
　　　　　　　　　　　　　　　(What time?)

_____ . We will stay there for about
　　　　　　　　　　(How?)

_____ hours. We plan to do the following things
　　　　(How long?)

there: _____

_____

_____ .

Then, _____

_____

_____

_____ .

We will return to school at _____ .
　　　　　　　　　　　　　　　　　　(What time?)

　Please tell us what you think.

---

*RE is for "regarding." After RE, write a word or phrase telling what the memo is about.

Grammar Appendix

Contents

1-E   *CAN/CAN'T*

> You **can see** films in a movie theater.
> We **can't buy** food in a hardware store.
>
> Use *can* and *can't (cannot)* to express ability and possibility. The simple form of the verb (*see*, *buy*, and so on) follows *can* and *can't*.

Use *can* and *can't* to make sentences about the places in the pictures.

1. (rent a car/rent a bike)

   We *can't rent a car* here,

   but we *can rent a bike*.

2. (buy flowers/get food)

   You *can buy flowers* in this shop,

   but you *can't get food*.

3. (see farms/see skyscrapers)

   We *can't see farms* in the city,

   but we *can see skyscrapers*.

4. (make noise/look at paintings)

   I *can't make noise* in a museum,

   but I *can look at paintings*.

5. (buy women's shoes/get men's shoes)

   You *can't get men's shoes* here,

   but you *can buy women's shoes*.

2-D   *THERE IS/THERE ARE*

There is a beautiful lake.	**There are** beautiful lakes.
There's a nice tree.	**There are** nice trees.

Use *there is (there's)* before singular words and *there are* before plural words in written English. In spoken English, *there's* is sometimes used with plural words too.

Colette is talking to her sister Gaby on the phone. Colette wants Gaby to join her at this hotel. Complete the sentences with *there is (there's)* or *there are*.

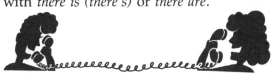

Colette: You really should come and see this hotel. It's beautiful!
Gaby: Oh, really? Does it have a pool?

Colette: No, but __*there's*__ a lake right next to it.
            1

Gaby: Hmmm. I like pools better.

Colette: But _____ boats on the lake. We can rent one if we want.
                    2

Gaby: Are there flowers and trees in the area?

Colette: Not many flowers, but _____ pine trees everywhere.
                                          3
            You'll love the pine scent.
Gaby: I prefer the smell of flowers. What about the hotel? Is it big?

Colette: _____ eight floors. And my room is on the top one.
                4

            _____ a great view!
                5
Gaby: Oh. I don't like heights. What about the food?

Colette: _____ two good restaurants. Come on, Gaby!
                6

            _____ a train tomorrow morning.
                7
Gaby: I'll think about it.
Colette: Oh, you're impossible!

3-F   *(IT) HAS/(IT) DOESN'T HAVE*

Can you tell me about the apartment?
It has big rooms and big windows.
It doesn't have a garage though.

In American English, the negative of
has is *doesn't have*.

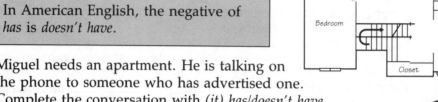

Miguel needs an apartment. He is talking on
the phone to someone who has advertised one.
Complete the conversation with *(it) has/doesn't have.*

Miguel: How big is the apartment?

Landlord: __It has__ five rooms and one big bathroom. And
             _1_
             there are three closets.

Miguel: How many bedrooms?

Landlord: Only one, I'm afraid, but it's big, and __It has__
             _2_
             a great view of the lake.

Miguel: Is there a big closet in the bedroom?

Landlord: __It doesn't have__ a closet.
             _3_

Miguel: No closet? What would I do with my clothes? Is there a big kitchen?
           I spend my free time cooking.

Landlord: Well, this apartment __It doesn't have__ a very large kitchen.
             _4_

             But __It has__ a spacious dining room, where you'll
             _5_
             enjoy eating. And you'll love the living room.
             __It has__ big windows and lots of light.
             _6_

Miguel: Is there a garage for my car?

Landlord: No, sorry.

Miguel: Hmmm. So, __It doesn't have__ a garage or a big kitchen
             _7_
           or a closet in the bedroom. I don't think your place is quite right for
           me, but thank you anyway!

2. it has   3. It doesn't have   4. doesn't have   5. it has   6. It has   7. it doesn't have

4-D VERB AGREEMENT WITH SINGULAR AND PLURAL SUBJECTS

Singular Subjects **A dessert is** good with dinner.	*Plural Subjects* **The desserts are** delicious! **They're** not expensive.
There **is a baked potato** on the menu.	**Are** there **potatoes** in the stew?
Is there **ice cream**? Yes, **today's ice cream is** lemon.	Noncount nouns stay in the singular.

Singular noun subjects take singular verbs; plural noun subjects take plural verbs. Noncount nouns take singular verbs.

Read the following conversation between a customer and a waiter at Ponte's Restaurant. Circle the appropriate verb in each item.

1. Customer: The menu says "vegetarian" stew. It *has/have* no meat, right?

2. Waiter: Correct. Our stew *is/are* meatless. There *is/are* eight vegetables in it—carrots, mushrooms, pota—

3. Customer: I'll think about it. *Is/Are* the spaghetti at Ponte's also vegetarian?

4. Waiter: Yes, it *comes/come* with a tomato sauce, not a meat sauce.

5. Customer: I'd like an appetizer. *Is/Are* the chips good?

6. Waiter: Yes, *it's/they're* delicious, and the shrimp cocktail *is/are* also excellent.

7. Customer: And expensive. Let's see. *Is/Are* there mineral water?

8. Waiter: Yes, and there *is/are* soft drinks too.

   Customer: Well, I'll have a baked potato and some tea—no, please bring me a fruit cup and coffee—no, no, no, make that a piece of cherry pie and a glass of water.

   Waiter: ###$%!!!###★!

5-D   SIMPLE PRESENT

I				
You	**play** baseball on Sundays.	He	**plays** baseball on Sundays.
We	**swim** in the summer.	She	**swims** in the summer.
They				

Use the simple present to talk or write about activities that are habitual or repeated.

It **snows** in the Rocky Mountains.

Also, use the simple present for general truths.

Lily and Jeff are sister and brother. They both love sports. Look at their bedrooms and tell what sports they do.

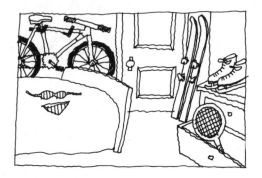

Lily's room   Jeff's room

1. Lily and Jeff both *ride bikes* _____.

2. They also _____ and _____.

3. In addition, Jeff _____ and _____.

4. Lily _____ and _____.

SIMPLE PRESENT: Negative Statements

I
You **don't play** baseball.   He **doesn't play** baseball.
We **don't like** to jog.   She **doesn't like** to jog.
They

Look back at the pictures on the opposite page. Write five negative sentences about Lily and/or Jeff using this chart.

Lily Lily and Jeff Jeff	don't doesn't	play soccer. ice-skate. ski. play Ping-Pong. lift weights. ride horses. swim.

1. <u>*Lily doesn't play soccer*</u> .
2. _____ .
3. _____ .
4. _____ .
5. _____ .
6. _____ .

SIMPLE PRESENT: Questions

I
Do you swim often?   Does he swim often?
   we   she
   they

Ask questions about Lily and/or Jeff.

7. 66 **Does Lily swim often?** 99
   66 **Yes, she swims every day.** 99

8. 66 _____ ? 99
   66 **Yes, he skis very well.** 99

9. 66 _____ ? 99
   66 **Yes, they do.** 99

10. 66 _____ ? 99
    66 **No, she doesn't play soccer, but she plays tennis.** 99

2-6. Jeff doesn't ice-skate. Lily and Jeff don't play Ping-Pong. Lily doesn't lift weights. Lily and Jeff don't ride horses. Jeff doesn't swim.
8. Does Jeff ski?
9. Do Jeff and Lily ski, play tennis, ride bikes?
10. Does Lily play soccer?

6-G   THE IMPERATIVE

> **Save** the planet!
> **Don't destroy** it!

Use the imperative to give someone advice, suggestions, or directions. Use the simple form of the verb. For the negative, put *do not* or *don't* in front of the verb.
(Note: Pronouns come after the verb.)

The Environmental Protection Agency has this slogan* about the earth: *If you want to save it, find out what you are doing to destroy it.* Below, tell people how they can destroy the earth. Fill in the blanks with one of these verbs.

* a phrase or sentence

drive	throw
buy	use
pour	recycle
fix	turn off

How to Destroy the Earth

1. _Throw_____ garbage into lakes and rivers.

2. _____ your car everywhere!

3. _____ lights in a room when you leave it.

4. _____ your aluminum cans.

5. _____ leaks in your faucets.

6. _____ lots of plastic cups and bags.

7. _____ your used motor oil on the ground.

7-E   *BOTH OF* AND *NEITHER OF*

John is quiet. I'm quiet.
Both of us are quiet.

Renata isn't lazy. Natasha isn't lazy.
Neither of them is (*or* are) lazy.

When we compare two people or things, we can use *both of* (with affirmative ideas) and *neither of* (with negative ideas). A plural verb follows *both of*. A singular verb usually follows *neither of*, but a plural verb is also possible.

Compare these people using *both of* or *neither of*.

1. Carla isn't weak.
    Superwoman isn't weak.

    Neither of them is weak .

2. Michael Jackson is rich.
    Mona is rich.

    _____ .

3. Troy doesn't swim.
    Peter doesn't swim.

    _____ .

4. I am hardworking.
    Carla is hardworking.

    _____ .

5. Carlos doesn't like soccer.
    Gladys doesn't like soccer.

    _____ .

6. I wasn't stupid.
    Einstein wasn't stupid.

    _____ .

7. Wu likes to talk.
    Rada likes to talk.

    _____ .

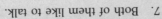

2. Both of them are rich.	4. Both of us are hardworking.
3. Neither of them swims (swim).	5. Neither of them likes (like) soccer.
6. Neither of us was (were) stupid.	
7. Both of them like to talk.	

7-E   PRESENT CONTINUOUS

It's eight o'clock.

I **am**   (**I'm**)   **studying** now.
You **are** (**You're**) **cooking** dinner.
He **is**   (**He's**)   **setting** the table.
We **are** (**We're**) all **working**, but
they **are** (**they're**) just **relaxing**!

The verbs in the sentences above are *active* or *action* verbs. With these verbs, the present continuous tells about activities happening now, at the moment of speaking.

I'm setting the table in a few minutes.
We're relaxing tonight. We're tired.

Sometimes the speaker feels very sure or strong about activities in the future. Then the present continuous can also be used.

What differences can you find in these pictures? Write sentences using the present continuous.

A

B

In A, Mr. Chin is sweeping. In B, he's vacuuming. .

_____ .

_____ .

_____ .

_____ .

In A, Ms. Chin is dusting the TV. In B, she's dusting a picture.
In A, Tim is mopping the floor. In B, he's washing the windows.
In A, Ying is washing a car. In B, she's washing a bike.
In A, Sue is walking a small dog. In B, she's walking a big one.

PRESENT CONTINUOUS: Questions and Negative Statements
Refer to picture A on page 110.

What **is** Mr. Chin **doing**?
Why **are** the Chins **cleaning** the house?

Note how questions are formed in the present continuous.

Mr. Chin **is not sitting** around.
He**'s not relaxing**.
He **isn't reading**.
The kids **aren't sitting** around either.
Everybody**'s working**.

Note how the negative present continuous is formed. The short forms are used mostly in speaking.

Look at picture A on page 110. Then complete each sentence using the correct form of the verb in parentheses.

1. The Chin family _*isn't playing*_ .
   (play)
   Then what _*are they doing*_ ?
   (do)
   They _*'re doing*_ the household chores!
   (do)

2. Tim _____ the garbage.
   (take out)
   Then what _____ ?
   (do)
   He _____ the floor.
   (wash)

3. Ms. Chin _____ television.
   (watch)
   Then what _____ ?
   (do)
   She _____ the television.
   (dust)

4. Ying and Sue _____ in the park.
   (play)
   Then what _____ ?
   (do)
   They _____ outside.
   (work)

8-F   SIMPLE PAST AND ADVERBS OF FREQUENCY

Vlado now lives alone, and he has to do all his chores by himself. He misses his two roommates Paul and Chan. Can you see why?

Regular Verbs	Irregular Verbs
Paul *always* **shopped** for groceries, Chan *often* **cooked** dinner, Vlado *never* **washed** the dishes,	and he *sometimes* **made** the beds too. and he *usually* **set** the table. and he *never* **took** out the garbage either.
Regular verbs have **-ed** in the past (*cooked* and *washed*). Sometimes they have a small spelling change (*shopped*). Some other regular verbs are dust–dusted repair–repaired iron–ironed vacuum–vacuumed mop–mopped walk–walked	Irregular verb forms need to be memorized. Some other irregular verbs are do–did make–made get–got set–set have–had take–took
always 100% of the time **usually** ↑ **often** 50% of the time **sometimes** ↓ **never** 0% of the time	*Always, usually, often, sometimes,* and *never* are called adverbs. They tell "how often." Use them before the main verb, as in the examples above. However, when the main verb is *be,* put the adverb after (*Vlado is often lazy*).

Complete the story about Vlado and his former roommates. Use an appropriate adverb and the correct past form of the verb.

Last year when Vlado, Paul, and Chan lived together, Chan

usually _____ *mopped* _____ the floors. He _____
1 (90% of the time)   (mop)   2   (50%)

_____ the rooms too. Chan _____ _____ dinner,
vacuum   3   (100%)   (cook)

and he _____ _____ the dishes. Paul _____
4   (25%)   (wash)   5   (90%)

_____ for groceries. Also, he _____ _____ the garbage and
(shop)   6   (50%)   (take out)

_____ the table too. Vlado _____ _____ any work in
7   (set)   8   (0%)   (do)

the kitchen. He _____ _____ busy—but not with household chores!
9   (be)   (100%)

SIMPLE PAST: Negative Statements

 Ali dusted all his records yesterday, but he **didn't dust** his bookshelves.

For negative statements in the past, use *did not* or *didn't* with the simple form of the verb.

Look at each picture. Then complete the unfinished sentence with a negative statement as in the example.

1. Yesterday Mr. Pike vacuumed the living room, but

   he didn't vacuum _____ the bedrooms.

2. Ms. Mundy took out the garbage on Tuesday, but

   _____ it out on Saturday.

3. Paul and Liang washed their car yesterday,

   but _____ *my* car!

4. Anna cooked a delicious dinner on Saturday, but last

   night _____ a very good dinner.

5. On Sunday, the children did the dishes after lunch,

   but _____ them after dinner.

6. Harry shopped for fresh fruits and vegetables yesterday,

   but _____ for milk and bread.

2. she didn't take
3. they didn't wash
4. she didn't cook
5. they didn't do
6. he didn't shop

9-E   *SHOULD/SHOULDN'T*

Mark smokes two packs of cigarettes a day.
He **shouldn't** smoke.
"I **should** stop," he thinks.

Should expresses a "good idea." The simple form of the verb (*smoke, stop*) follows *should*. *Should* always has the same form (*I should stop, you should stop, she should stop, we should stop, they should stop*). The negative form is *should not* or *shouldn't*.

Notice how *should* is used in questions:	**Should** Mark **give up** cigarettes? Why **should** Mark **stop**?

Below, Mark and Eric are giving advice to their friend Rosa, who doesn't feel well. Complete their conversation. Use *should* or *shouldn't* with the verbs in the box.

call	come	stay	drink	go	eat	take

Rosa: I have such a miserable cold!

Mark: Rosa, you ___*should stay*___ in bed. And you _____
     1   2
   a lot of tea with lemon and honey.

Eric: No. I don't think tea is so good for a cold. My grandmother says you

   _____ chicken soup. It'll cure you. And I think you
       3

   _____ out and get some fresh air. You _____ in bed, Rosa!
       4   5

Rosa: Hmmm. Thanks for the great advice, guys. What about medicine?

   _____ I _____ vitamin C or aspirin or anything?
       6

Mark: Maybe. I suppose you _____ the clinic and ask.
                      7

Eric: Also, movies are very good for colds. You _____
   to the movies with me tonight, Rosa!   8

Rosa: You're crazy, Eric! I _____ you seriously.
                    9

10-G   *BECAUSE* AND *SO*

Jorge needs towels **because** he takes a lot of showers.
Jorge takes a lot of showers, **so** he needs towels.

We can use *because* or *so* to connect two ideas that have a cause-effect relationship. *Because* introduces the cause idea and answers the question, *Why? So* introduces the effect idea. Notice the comma before *so*.

Sue and Ngo are discussing birthday gifts for their good friends, Jill and Joel, who are twins. Fill in the blanks with *because* or, *so*.

Sue: We have to get something for Jill and Joel ___*because*___ their
1
birthday is coming up next week.

Ngo: Well, Jill loves sweets ___*so*___ why don't we buy her a box
2
of chocolates?

Sue: Well, she doesn't eat sweets anymore _____ she's on a
3

diet. But she travels a lot _____ an atlas might be a good
4
idea.

Ngo: No. She probably has one already. How about flowers?

Sue: Good idea. She likes tulips _____ let's get her a dozen
yellow ones. Now, what about Joel?   5

Ngo: How about a watch? I think he needs a new one _____
6
he's always late.

Sue: You're right, but a watch is too expensive. I don't have much money

_____ let's think of something cheaper.
7

Ngo: OK. I know. A Madonna tape! It's perfect _____ he loves
her music, and it's cheap!

Sue: Great idea!

3. because
4. , so
5. , so
6. because
7. , so
8. because

11-C   GERUNDS AS SUBJECTS

> a.   **Laughing** is good for you.
> b.   **Going to the movies** is expensive.
> c.   **Singing and dancing** are fun.

A *gerund* is a noun made from a verb (VERB +*ing*). In these examples, gerunds and gerund phrases are the *subjects* of the sentences. Gerund subjects take singular verbs (as in *a* and *b*) and plural verbs when they are compound (as in *c*).

Fill in the blanks with a gerund or gerund phrase. Circle a singular or plural verb as appropriate.

1.   *Buying a new car* _____ (is)/*are* very expensive.
     (buy a new car)

2.   _____ *doesn't*/*don't* cost a thing.
     (sing)

3.   _____ *is*/*are* popular free-time
     (watch TV and read)
     activities.

4.   _____ at McDonald's *is*/*are*
     (eat out)
     inexpensive.

5.   _____ during the day *is*/*are* often
     (go to the movies)
     cheaper than at night.

6.   _____ *is*/*are* big monthly
     (pay rent and buy food)
     expenses for most people.

7.   _____ *costs*/*cost* nothing, and it's
     (play baseball)
     fun!

8.   _____ *is*/*are* hard work!
     (read schoolbooks)

12-E   *HAS TO/HAVE TO AND CAN*

> Students **have to study** a lot, but they **don't have to study** all the time. They **can have fun** with their friends too.
>
> Use *has to/have to* to express obligation and necessity. The negative is *doesn't/don't have to.*
>
> Use *can* to express possibility and ability. See page 102 for an explanation and exercises with *can* and *can't.*

Mark and his friend Ellen are talking about jobs for Mark. Complete their conversation with *has to, have to, doesn't have to, don't have to,* or *can.*

Ellen: Mark, you _____*can*_____ get a job as a waiter.
                              1

Mark: No, waiters _____ be on their feet all day. It's tiring.
                              2

Ellen: No, they _____ stand up all the time.
                              3

They _____ sit down during breaks. But if you like to sit
            4

so much, why don't you get a job as a cashier at Wolf's Cafeteria? You

_____ sit down all day there!
      5

Mark: Yes, but a cashier _____ count money. That's boring. I'd
                              6

like an exciting job—like police officer.

Ellen: Are you sure? My brother is a police officer in Denver. He

_____ work at night. And it's dangerous.
      7

Mark: Well, I just need a part-time job anyway. Here's an ad for a job. Monty's Restaurant needs a dishwasher.

Ellen: My friend Lucia works there. She _____ scrub lots of pots
                                          8
and pans. Does that sound like fun?

Mark: But she _____ wash everything by
                              9

hand, does she? The machines _____ wash the plates
                                                10
and glasses. I think I'll apply today!

10. can
9. doesn't
   have to
8. has to
7. has to
6. has to
5. can
4. can
3. don't
   have to
2. have to

13-G   *VERY* AND *TOO*

> a. The weather is **very** cold, but I'll walk to work.
> b. The weather is **too** cold. I can't walk to work.
>   The weather is **too** cold for me to walk to work.

Very and *too* do not mean the same thing. In sentence a, the weather is uncomfortable, but it is still possible to walk to work. In the sentences in b, it is impossible. *Too* has a negative meaning.

Fill in the blanks with *very* or *too*.

1. It's ___*very*___ hot in my country in the summer; I love it! But

    sometimes it's ___*too*___ hot to stay in the sun.

2. It's _____ cool to go to the beach today. Let's go tomorrow.

    They say the weather is going to be _____ warm.

3. Montreal is _____ cold in the wintertime, and skiing and ice

    skating are popular sports. Winter there is _____ cold for my
    parents though. They prefer to go to Florida and swim.

4. I'd like to take a photo, but it's _____ cloudy. My film is
    only for bright sunshine. The weather changed so fast! It

    was _____ sunny and beautiful an hour ago.

5. My winter coat is _____ big to fit in my suitcase. Will I need

    it? Is it _____ cold in Seattle in the winter?

14-D ORDER OF ADJECTIVES

That's a **nice** tie!
Harry was wearing a **nice striped** tie.
But he had on an **ugly black** shirt.

You know that adjectives come before nouns in English. Sometimes there are two or more adjectives together. **Opinion** adjectives usually go before **fact** adjectives. (*Nice* and *ugly* are opinions; *striped* and *black* are facts.)

It's a **nice long black printed** skirt.

In this exercise, you use three kinds of fact adjectives. They are usually in this order:

SIZE + COLOR + MATERIAL
(*long*)   (*black*)   (*printed*)

Write sentences describing these clothes. Put the adjectives in the correct order.

1. aqua
good-looking
checked

It's a good-looking aqua checked shirt.

2. black-and-white
printed
stylish

3. ugly
polka-dotted
black

4. black
wide

5. striped
aqua
wild

2. It's a stylish black-and-white printed sweater.
3. It's an ugly black polka-dotted skirt.
4. They're wide black pants.
5. It's a wild aqua striped tie.

15-E   INFINITIVES OF PURPOSE

People go to a stadium **to watch** a game.
(*People go to a stadium because they want to watch a game.*)

I went to the police station **to report** a robbery.
(*I went to the police station because I wanted to report a robbery.*)

Use the infinitive (*to watch, to report*) to tell *why* someone does or did something.

Fill in each blank with a phrase beginning with an infinitive of purpose. Choose from the verb phrases on the right.

1. People visit a zoo _to see_

   animals .

2. I go to English class _____

   _____ .

3. The stopped at the post office _____

   _____ .

4. People go to a movie theater _____

   _____ .

5. I went to the bank _____

   _____ .

6. Ming stopped at the library _____

   _____ .

7. Jon made an appointment at the

   health clinic _____ .

8. Many people go to department

   stores _____

   _____ .

see a movie
get some books
learn English
buy furniture
cash a check
see animals
get some stamps
see a doctor

2. to learn English
3. to get some stamps
4. to see a movie
5. to cash a check
6. to get some books
7. to see a doctor
8. to buy furniture

15-J   FUTURE WITH *WILL*

> I **will be** (**I'll be**) late for work tomorrow.
> My boss **won't be** happy about that.

One way to talk about future plans in English is by using *will* + the simple form of the verb. In everyday English, *will* is usually contracted to *'ll* with pronouns (*I'll, you'll, he'll, they'll*). The negative is *won't* (or *will not* in formal or emphatic usage).

It's Friday morning. Dong has just arrived at work, but he's already thinking about his Saturday plans. Fill in each blank with a verb in future time. Use the verbs below.

watch	have	be
go	ride	visit
meet		

In the morning, he **'ll   visit**_____ the zoo with his nephew.
1

Afterward, they _____ to Seabreeze Amusement Park. Dong
2

likes the Ferris wheel, but he _____ the roller coaster because
3

it makes him sick. In the evening, he _____ his friend Lee,
4

and they _____ dinner at a Chinese restaurant. When he gets
5

home, he _____ tired. He _____ TV and fall
6   7

asleep.

Answer Appendix

Contents

2-J **SAMPLE POSTCARD**

La Jolla
July 16

Dear Barbara,
Our beach house is wonderful!
It's small and simple, but
it has a great view of the
ocean. There's a little porch,
where we eat breakfast and
lunch. It's peaceful. I
don't want to leave
this paradise!
Regards,
Tomo

Sunburst Graphics, 105 Eastland Avenue, Midway, CA 99999

Sunburst Graphics © 1991

U.S.A. 19¢

Ms. Barbara Shain
2163 South Rose Street
Pocatello, ID 83201

3-B ANSWERS

1. The pool is _behind_ the house.

2. The dining room is _between_ the kitchen and the living room.

3. The family room is _in the front of_ the house.

4. The bedroom is _next to_ the hallway.

5. The driveway is _in the front of_ the house.

6. The dining room is _in the back of_ the house.

3-C ANSWERS

1. The kitchen looks out on _the woods_.

2. The family room looks out on _First Avenue_.

3. The living room looks out on _Green Street_ and _the pool_.

4. The big bathroom looks out on _the woods_.

5. The bedroom looks out on _Green Street_ and _First Avenue_.

3-H   **SAMPLE PROJECT NOTES**

PROJECT: *My Dream House*

Write your name(s) here. — ARCHITECT(S): *Yannis Kamaritis*

Put a number here. —

Mention any special feature such as size or location here. —

4	**BEDROOMS** Notes: *2 large and 2 small*
4	**BATHROOMS** Notes: *1 bathroom next to each bedroom*
2	**– CAR GARAGE** Notes: *Behind the house*
1	**KITCHEN** Notes: *Very large with a fireplace*
8	**CLOSETS** Notes: *Big!*

1	**FAMILY ROOM** Notes: *Small and cozy with fireplace*
1	**DINING ROOM** Notes: *Next to kitchen*
1	**LIVING ROOM** Notes: *Large with skylight*
1	**OTHER (a)** *Exercise room* Notes: *Large with many windows*
1	**OTHER (b)** *Porch* Notes: *Behind the house*

4–1   **ANSWERS**

APPETIZERS

tomato soup
soup of the day
shrimp cocktail

ENTREES

curried chicken
chopped steak
fried rice with shrimp
spaghetti with clam sauce
vegetarian chili

Menu

VEGETABLES

mashed potatoes
carrots
broccoli
Cuban black beans

DESSERTS

apple pie
strawberry ice cream
cheesecake
banana cream pie

BEVERAGES

soft drinks
apple juice
iced tea
mineral water

5-E　ANSWERS

swimming

tennis

Ping-Pong

walking

soccer

baseball

volleyball

karate

aerobics

basketball

weight lifting

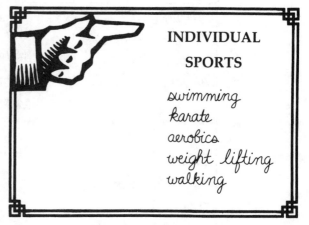

INDIVIDUAL SPORTS

swimming
karate
aerobics
weight lifting
walking

TEAM SPORTS

tennis
Ping-Pong
soccer
baseball
volleyball
basketball

7-C **ANSWERS**

TALKATIVE   rich   POOR   serious

STRONG   **hardworking**

FUNNY   weak   **insensitive**

unromantic   lazy   **romantic**   sensitive

quiet   sad   cheerful

rich / poor	romantic / unromantic
strong / weak	funny / serious
quiet / talkative	insensitive / sensitive
sad / cheerful	lazy / hardworking

8–C   **ANSWERS**

MAKING COFFEE

TAKING A SHOWER

setting the table

doing homework

making the bed

cleaning the bathroom

mowing the lawn

SWIMMING

ironing

TALKING ON THE PHONE

repairing the sink

sweeping the floor

changing a light bulb

washing the windows

getting dressed

reading the newspaper

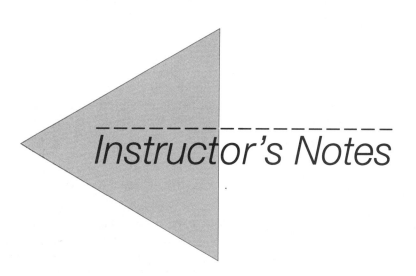

Instructor's Notes

Please see ABOUT THIS BOOK for general guidelines and suggestions for using this text. These INSTRUCTOR'S NOTES offer specific suggestions for individual activities as well as *Extension Activities* for each lesson, *Quiz Ideas*, and *Cross-Cultural Focus* activities. Since key activities in the text make use of group work, some general ideas for facilitating group work will be offered first.

FORMING GROUPS: Decide before class how students will be grouped for the culminating group problem-solving activity. You may decide to allow groups to form naturally according to where students seat themselves or according to the principles of friendliness. You may decide, however, that some teacher guidance is necessary to avoid the common problem of students sticking together by nationality (and thus speaking the first language) and to encourage students to interact with each and every peer. Although mixed-ability groups work very well, with the stronger learners helping and modeling the language for the less fluent ones, there may also be a time and place for grouping students according to ability level. Such an arrangement will allow more advanced students to feel challenged and less advanced ones to take control and not feel intimidated. You might try, then, to vary the

groups from time to time (but not necessarily every class period) to keep the interactions fresh and to allow for exposure to different students, ideas, and types of learning. If you decide to compose the groups yourself, one of the following techniques might help set them up.

· Write students' names in groups on the board. These groups can be sketched out before class—with an eye to mixing abilities, nationalities, or sexes—and put on the board as class begins.

· Form random or selected groups by handing out slips of paper with different colors (four blue, four green, and so on) and have students with the same color form a group.

Students can get into groups as they enter the classroom, if you wish (even though the group activity will not occur until later), as this will eliminate the need for reshuffling in the middle of the class and will make the search for a pair-work partner easier, since each group of four can simply divide into two pairs. If the class does not divide evenly into fours, groups of three or five will also work well. With very small classes, pairs may be able to do the group work.

PROMOTING PARTICIPATION AND RESPONSIBILITY WITHIN GROUPS: One way to ensure everyone's participation within the groups is to have each group member assume one of the following roles.

1. Leader: It is the leader's responsibility to make sure that everyone contributes something in the discussion. The leader is in charge of maintaining group harmony.

2. Timer: The timer needs to keep track of the time (assuming a time limit has been given) and keep the group "on task."

3. Recorder: The recorder keeps a few notes on the discussion and reads back the ideas to the group periodically.

4. Reporter: The reporter knows what the group's consensus is and reports it back to the class.

In cases where the groups have fewer than four members, the roles can be combined.

   Another way to ensure that all members of a group will participate, and that no one will dominate, is to issue tokens such as coins, buttons, or beads to each member of the group. The exact number you issue will depend on how complex the group task is, but in general, five or six tokens per student should suffice. Tell students that each time they take a turn, they must put a token in the cup/jar/box you provide. All tokens must be used up during the task.

KEEPING STUDENTS SPEAKING ENGLISH: During group work, students sometimes lapse into their native language. This tendency will be minimized if you stress that the classroom is an English-only environment. For added emphasis, try one of the following techniques.

• At the beginning of the course, have students sign a contract that specifies their responsibility to speak only English.

• Try instituting a fine for the use of students' native language(s). This can be done in a playful way; bring in a piggy bank and announce to students that each time they speak their native language, they must contribute a small set amount of money to the bank. Tell them how the collected money will be used (for a class party, a selected charity, and so on).

• At the beginning of the group activity, hand each group one token. Explain that when a group member lapses into his or her native tongue, he or she must take the token. Whoever has it at the end of the activity must treat the rest of the group to a drink, a piece of candy, or some other small treat.

COMING TO A CONSENSUS: The goal of each problem-solving activity is having each group reach a consensus after the discussion of a topic. Students may need help in understanding how this can be achieved. Tell them that they should listen carefully to one another's ideas to determine which point of view they find most convincing. After hearing a particularly persuasive point of view, group members may all take the same side. If, however, group members continue to disagree, a vote should be taken and the majority view adopted as the group's view.

1   IMPROVE YOUR HOMETOWN

1-A   Students can work individually or in pairs. Suggest to students that they write the names of the places under the pictures (or write the appropriate letter next to each name). Then ask, "What's in Picture A?" "B?" and so on. Point out that we say "*It's a zoo*," but "*It's an art museum*."

1-C Students can work individually or in pairs. You may want to go over some of the more difficult words and phrases (for example, *jog, relax, keep fit*) first, eliciting meanings from students if possible. Or, tell students that they can use their dictionaries and/or, if you prefer, you as a ready resource and have them plunge right into the activity.

QUIZ IDEA: Students could be asked to study this vocabulary at home in preparation for a quiz that could take one of several forms: (1) an oral quiz in which students would take turns answering questions such as "What can you do in a library?" (2) a listening-dictation quiz for which students would write sentences that you dictate based on the vocabulary, or (3) a written fill-in-the-blank quiz, which could parallel the activity in 1–C (you might simply choose two or three incomplete sentences from the activity and write them on the board).

1-D Explain that one student will invite and the other refuse. Ask one pair of students to model the example. Then ask the same pair to talk about the art museum, making the necessary changes in the dialog. Once the students' task seems clear, instruct each student to invite the other to three different places.

1-E Refer students who need further work with *can* and *can't* to the GRAMMAR APPENDIX, page 102.

1-F (See page 131 for suggestions about how to group students.) Present the problem by reading it aloud or paraphrasing it. Discuss the first item (zoo) with the whole class. Then give groups five or ten minutes for further discussion. Allow the groups at least a few minutes to share their ideas with the class. The aim of this activity is to prime students for the discussion in 1–G as well as to get them to think critically about certain age groups in society and the differing benefits these groups may reap from various public facilities.

You might also want to address the issue of how frequently each facility will be used.

1-G
1-H Since this is the first group problem-solving activity in the book, students may need help to get started. (See the suggestions for group work on page 132.) Direct students' attention to the *Helpful Language* section, pointing out that they can use some of these phrases in their discussion. Students will benefit from hearing the phrases and sentences spoken and then repeating them. Set a time limit of about ten minutes for groups to complete the activity. You can write the end time on the board or set a timer to ring when time is up. While students are discussing, circulate to offer help and encouragement, but keep in mind that your presence in a group may intimidate some students and keep them from saying what they would say to a peer. Some implicit error correction may be appropriate here, but refrain from explicit correction. If students would like to do some follow-up work on accuracy, consider tape-recording one or two groups during a problem-solving session and then discussing parts of the recording in an office conference or in class, if the participants are willing. The tape might also be given to the participants to transcribe and correct at home.

1-I After individual groups have reached a consensus, regroup the class for a quick "debriefing" of the problem so that groups can exchange their decisions/solutions. This sharing will give the groups a feeling that their conclusions are important and that their discussions had a purpose. Have several groups write their choices on the board. Encourage students to compare their choices and to justify them.

1–J   This writing activity can be done in class, if time permits, or as homework. Ask students to write on their own paper. Students might enjoy reading their peers' reports; pairing students with partners who were not in their original groups would work best.

EXTENSION ACTIVITY: Have students write and then talk about their favorite place(s) to go in their free time. Have them explain what they can do in these places.

2   RENT A VACATION HOME

2–A   Make sure that students know what a lottery is and why congratulations are in order. Ask students if they'd like to take a vacation with their lottery money. Then ask them to look at the photos on the page. Ask, "What do all the photos have in common?" Explain that these are all vacation houses advertised for rent in a newspaper. Then give students five minutes or so to work individually or in pairs to find adjectives to match each house. (Students can write the appropriate adjectives under each photo.) Then ask, "Can you describe the beach house?" "Can you describe the country house?" and so on. See if students agree with the descriptions of their peers.

You might wish to put other relevant descriptive adjectives on the board at this point and ask students which house or houses the words describe. These might include *cozy, isolated/centrally located, bright/ dark,* and *comfortable/uncomfortable.*

2–B   Ask students to talk to a partner for a moment about which house they prefer. Then ask, for example, "Gloria, which house does Faheed prefer?" "Why?" "What can he do there?"

2–C   Tell students that Ji Young is dreaming about renting this vacation house. Direct their attention to the example sentences with *It has,* perhaps pointing out the use of the article *a* with singular count nouns. Students can write more sentences either on their own or in pairs. When they finish, have some of the sentences written on the board. Allow peers to correct each other where necessary.

2–D   Refer students who need further work with *There is* and *There are* to the GRAMMAR APPENDIX, page 103.

2–E   *EXTENSION ACTIVITY:* Additional in-class practice with *There is* and *There are* can be given with the following game: Arrange students in pairs or small groups. Put a variety of objects that students can name in English (pens, a book, keys, an apple, a watch, cassettes, dollars, and so on) on a tray. Go around the room, showing the contents on the tray to each group for several seconds. Then hide the tray and say, "What's on the tray? Together, write sentences. The group with the most true sentences when I say, 'Stop' wins." After several minutes, tell students to stop and find out who has written the most sentences. That group should read their sentences aloud, one by one. The other groups judge the responses for truth and accuracy and decide for each sentence whether a point should be given. If this group has not won all potential points, there may be another group that can challenge the original group.

2-F The aims of this activity are: (1) to give students further linguistic practice with *It has/It doesn't have* and *There is/There are*, (2) to get students to practice the critical thinking skill of seeing both sides of a question, and (3) to prime students with ideas and vocabulary for the group problem-solving activity that follows. When pairs finish writing, have them share some of their ideas with the class. This can be done orally or on the board. The class should focus first on the ideas presented and only later, if necessary, on form.

QUIZ IDEA: Tell students to study all the vocabulary in 2–A through 2–F as well as the structures *It has* and *There is/There are*. To test them in a rather open-ended fashion, ask them to look only at page 8. They should write one thing they like about each house. Each idea can be written in two ways—first with *It has*, and then with *There is* or *There are*.

2-G
2-H (See pages 131–132 for suggestions on how to manage group work.) Make sure students understand the task. Then have them repeat the *Helpful Language* after you. Give the groups a time limit of about ten minutes to complete their discussion and fill out 2–H.

2-I After individual groups have reached a consensus, it is valuable to regroup the class for a quick "debriefing" of the problem so that groups can exchange their decisions/solutions. This sharing will give the groups a feeling that their conclusions are important and that their discussions had a purpose. Have groups either report back orally or write the sentences from 2–H on the board.

2-J This activity can be done in class or as homework. Students may wish to read their cards to their peers before or after they are checked.

3 DESIGN A DREAM HOME

3-A Write the model sentence on the board: *We can usually find _____ in the _____ or _____.* Then ask, "Where can we usually find a telephone in a house?" Student 1 may answer, "In the kitchen!" Student 2 may add, "Also in the bedroom!" Ask the others if they agree and if they've seen phones in any other rooms in a house. Then go over the rest of the room names with students, eliciting information from those who know the meanings of the words (for example, "What do you usually do in a dining room?") Allow students to talk about the rest of the objects in pairs for five minutes or so before sharing a few of their ideas with the class.

3-B
3-C Students can do this activity individually or in pairs.

3-E After students have talked, ask, for example, "Figen, which house does your partner prefer? Why?"

3-F Refer students who need further work with *(It) has* and *(It) doesn't have* to the GRAMMAR APPENDIX, page 104.

3-G There are two options for this problem-solving task. Explain to students that they can design a house for a Hollywood star, Sally Star (option A), or they can design a dream home for themselves (option B). Get individuals who have chosen option B started first. Then have the remaining students form groups of two or three. They should be seated so that they can all see the drawing from the same angle. Go over the information about Sally Star with students. Elaborate on the first two pieces of information so that students get the gist of the activity.

YOU: She hates street noise and loves a view of the water. So how should you design the house?
S₁: It should look out on the pond!
S₂: No windows on Hollywood Boulevard!
YOU: OK. That would keep out some street noise.

Simply read the rest of the information aloud to see if there are any questions about vocabulary. Then have students repeat the *Helpful Language* after you. Students will probably need more time than usual to work out this problem, about twenty minutes. If you'd eventually like students to react to other groups' designs, you might consider bringing in large sheets of paper that students could draw on and that could be tacked up around the room.

3-H   Explain to students that architects often fill out notes such as these to accompany their designs. Have students look at the ANSWER APPENDIX, page 126, for a sample before they begin writing their notes.

EXTENSION ACTIVITY: Have students role-play, in pairs, a realtor and a person looking for an apartment or house. The client should describe what he or she is looking for in a home. The realtor should listen carefully and try to sketch the home, showing the rooms desired, their relative size, and so on.

4   PLAN YOUR PARTY MENU

4-A   Ask students to look first at the headings (*Appetizers, Entrees,* and so on) on the menu. Encourage them to use the layout and context to arrive at the meanings of any

unknown headings. Then have students look at the pictures under the menu. Ask them to try to find (individually or in pairs) the names for these items on the menu. They can write the appropriate words near each picture, if they wish.

Notice that some of the items on the menu are not pictured. Go over these items with students to make sure they are understood.

4-B   Give pairs a few minutes to discuss what foods on the menu they like and dislike. If students have the necessary language, encourage them to mention *any* foods they particularly like or dislike. Volunteers can then report on what their partners said.

EXTENSION ACTIVITY: Have students role-play waiter or waitress and customer in Ponte's Restaurant. They can practice in pairs, and volunteers can role-play for the class if time permits. Before pairs begin the role play, give students a dialog guide on the board.

WAITPERSON: Are you ready to order?
CUSTOMER: Yes, I'd like _____.
WAITPERSON: Anything to drink?
CUSTOMER: _____.
WAITPERSON: How about dessert?
CUSTOMER: _____.

4-C   Before pairs begin this activity, allow students a few minutes to practice saying prices. You could either write some figures on the board or have students look at the menu in 4-A. Ask, "How much is the tea?" (A/One dollar.) "the corn?" (A dollar fifty.) "the juice?" (Two dollars.) "the chocolate cake?" (Two fifty.) You might point out the longer and less common way to quote prices: *A dollar and fifty cents* and *Two dollars and twenty-five cents.* For this activity, students can refer to the note in 4-C, which writes the dollar amounts the way they are commonly said. Then model one or two items with a student to clarify to the class how this information-gap activity works.

4-D   Refer students who need work with verb agreement with singular and plural nouns to the GRAMMAR APPENDIX, page 105.

4-F   If time permits, ask a few pairs to write their lists on the board. See if there is agreement among the pairs who wrote on the board and then elicit opinions from the rest of the class. The objective of this activity is to encourage discussion; there are not many clear-cut right and wrong answers. Fish, for example, is generally healthful, but fish from some waters have a high mercury content. The cherries in cherry pie are healthful; the fat and sugar are not. Encourage students to see these gray areas.

EXTENSION ACTIVITY: Have students formulate questions concerning diet and health. Invite a dietician or health-care professional (perhaps a school nurse) to class to respond to the questions.

CROSS-CULTURAL FOCUS: If students are interested, have the class take a cross-cultural look at foods. Ask not only about the favorite foods and dishes in students' countries but also about the foods they do not eat. Point out that eating habits are not universal. You might take a poll, for example, of whether the following are eaten in students' countries: cows, sheep, horses, pigs, dogs, chickens, insects (grasshoppers, ants), and snails.

4-G   Make sure students understand the two criteria for the menu they select: (1) the menu should include things that everyone

likes, and (2) the cost should be $10.50 or under. Have students repeat the *Helpful Language* after you. Give the groups a time limit of about ten to fifteen minutes to complete their discussion and fill out the dinner menu.

4-I   Students can work individually or in pairs, at home or in class, on this activity. Many of the words that students are classifying here were seen in one form or another in 4–A. Instruct students to use dictionaries or ask you about words they haven't seen before. Students can check their categories in the ANSWER APPENDIX on page 127, if you don't want to take class time to do it.

5   ORGANIZE A SPORTS SCHEDULE

5-A
5-B   Students will be familiar with most of the sports depicted, though the English names for some may be less familiar. Give students a chance to hear your pronunciations of the names of these sports and encourage them to name other sports they know. You might let students know that another common name for Ping-Pong in English is *table tennis*.

CROSS-CULTURAL FOCUS: In many parts of the world, the sport we call *soccer* in the United States may be known as *football*. Have students talk about which sports are popular in their countries.

5-C   Student pairs should be able to follow the model in asking and making notes about a partner's sports habits. Have students help each other with any sports that may be unfamiliar.

5-E   Students can check their answers on page 128 in the ANSWER APPENDIX, and/or you can go over the solutions with the whole group. This classification between group and individual sports is needed in subsequent activities, so make sure everyone does this activity.

5-F   This question is intended to get students thinking about cross-cultural and cross-generational differences in sports participation. Remember that "popular" sports can be spectator sports or sports that people play.

5-G   This activity gives students a chance to practice writing sentences about different people's likes and dislikes in sports. Encourage students to think about the people they know as they complete the sentences. Make it clear that everyone can come up with different sentences. Students can share their ideas by trading books and/or by reading their sentences aloud to the class. Point out that we usually "play" sports involving a ball (or similar object, like a puck in hockey), for example, *play baseball* and *play football*. We do not "play" karate or aerobics; we "do" them.

5-H
5-I   This activity works best with three or four students, but pairs will also do. The task should be clear-cut. Remind students to refer to their classifications in 5-E and to their ideas in 5-G as they plan their evening schedules. Ideally you will have time either right after the activity or on the following day to have the group "reporters" put their completed schedules on the board so that students can compare and discuss reasons for their solutions.

5-J   Students can complete their information sheets in class or for homework.

EXTENSION ACTIVITY: Ask for student volunteers to do a survey by compiling the results of all the students' answers on the information sheets from 5-J. The results of the survey can be tabulated to put on a bulletin board or in a student newsletter.

6   SAVE THE PLANET

6-A   Use the visuals to introduce or elicit from students the meanings of *pollution* and *pollute*. While the noun form *pollution* has become very widespread, and may be a cognate or borrowed word in many students' languages, the verb *pollute* is less commonly used.

Most of the items in 6-A are intended as clear-cut examples of things that pollute (air conditioners, airplanes, spray cans, cars, factories, oil, ships, smoke, chemicals), or clear-cut examples of things—most of them occurring in nature—that do *not* themselves pollute (oceans, rivers, the sun, trees), but which can be affected *by* pollution. Another example, bicycles, does not pollute; rather, as an alternative to cars, bicycles can be seen as *reducing* pollution. However, some of the items are included as more ambiguous, problematic examples. Acid rain (see below) is both a *result* and a *cause* of pollution. People in industrial societies are the major indirect cause of pollution, but people in natural settings may not be polluters.

Note: *Acid rain* is rainwater affected by severe air pollution from highly industrial areas. It is a threat to plant and animal life. *Air conditioners* are hazardous because they are one of the products that use *chlorofluorocarbons,* or *CFCs,* which damage the ozone layer around the earth. *Spray cans* containing deodorant or paint, for example, also use CFCs.

6-B   Other things students may think of or you might want to suggest are disposable baby diapers; lack of trees and destruction of forests (plants can turn carbon dioxide into breathable oxygen; pesticides and many household soaps and products; plastic bags and plastic products in general; smog (the dark mixture of fog, smoke, and vehicle waste gases in the air in large cities of the world); and wood- and coal-burning.

6-E   This activity has students match an imperative verb phrase with an object phrase. Tell students there is one "best" match for each verb. Explain briefly *why* certain combinations they may come up with, for example, "Take your cans and bottles," are unmeaningful, ungrammatical, or unclear. In this case, it is not clear *where* the cans and bottles should be taken. Therefore, "Take a bus instead of a private car" is the preferred answer.

6-F   This activity allows students to follow up 6-E with a written exercise. You may want to remind them to use the imperative form. Have students who need practice with the imperative first do 6-G. Help students who need ideas come up with two additional suggestions by asking what other recycling, transportation, home energy use, or water conservation steps they can think of.

6-H   In this activity, students can use their various background experiences and information to add interesting examples to each of the four types of problems listed. Some examples for each are (1) Athens (Greece), Buenos Aires (Argentina), Mexico City, Denver (Colorado), New York City, Los Angeles, and Prague (Czecho-Slovakia); (2) the Rhine River and Lake Erie; (3) the

Adriatic Sea, the North Sea, and the Atlantic Ocean; (4) the Black Forest in southern Germany and Switzerland, in Poland, and in the Amazon area in South America.

6-I   *EXTENSION ACTIVITY:* Use a world map and/or a map of the United States and have students identify the different places mentioned here, or other places where there are environmental problems.

QUIZ IDEA: A short quiz can help students tie together some of the vocabulary and structures (imperative) introduced in the unit. One idea is to give a combination dictation/writing quiz. Before the quiz, write the verbs from 6-E on the board (*Turn off, Don't take, Recycle, Don't throw, Take, Don't buy*). Then dictate five sentences about pollution, such as "Garbage pollutes the land," using vocabulary and ideas from 6-A and/or 6-B. After students have written the dictated sentences, have them go back and write for each a related *imperative* sentence of their own, using the verbs on the board, for example, *Recycle your cans and bottles*. Other sample sentences for dictation are, *Cars pollute the air. Oil from ships pollutes the water. Burning coal pollutes the air. (Toxic) chemicals pollute the land.*

6-J   Make sure that each group understands that although they may consider all of the problems as serious, they must decide on *only one problem* to work on for this activity. For describing the problems and discussing their opinions, students can benefit from the *Helpful Language* on page 37. Read through the sample sentences and have students repeat or, if applicable, respond using the models provided.

6-L   There are several different ways that you might use this Writing Review. Working individually, students can complete the sentences, which form a short expository essay, in class or at home following the group activities in 6–J and 6–K. You can collect these, add your comments, and return them to the students. Or, using a writing process technique, have students exchange papers and read each other's essays; encourage them to write any comments about their partner's ideas or language in the margins. After returning papers and reading over comments, students can make any desired changes before handing the papers in. You can make an overhead transparency or a photocopy of one or two exemplary essays for the whole class to read together.

7 PLAY MATCHMAKER

7–A   Have students work individually or in pairs to match the adjectives and pictures. They can either write the appropriate letters next to the adjectives or the appropriate adjectives near the pictures. To check students' work, ask, "What word(s) describe the person in picture a? in b?" If students don't recognize Albert Einstein, Michael Jackson, or Charlie Chaplin, you might explain why each is famous.

7–B   Make sure that students understand the two different uses of *partner* in these instructions. Give pairs a few minutes to generate some ideas. Then see if there is a consensus in the class about the most important qualities in a partner/spouse.

Elicit other adjectives that students feel are important in a partner or spouse, for example: *adaptable, understanding, brave, neat, patient, good-natured,* and *thrifty*.

7–C   Students can work independently or in pairs on this activity.

7–D   To check students' writing, walk around the room as they work, offering guidance where necessary. Volunteers can put some of their sentences on the board.

7–E   *QUIZ IDEA:* Tell students to study the four ways of combining sentences that were presented in 7–D and 7–E. Then give them pairs of sentences similar to those they have been working with and have them connect the sentences with one of the following forms: *but, and . . . too, both of,* or *neither of*.

7–F   Give students a few minutes to rank these qualities. Ask pairs to share their rankings. Then elicit some opinions from the class. If students have the linguistic ability, ask them to give their reasons. Finally, you might take a poll to see which quality students feel is the most important in a partner. Tabulate the results on the board, allowing students to comment as they wish.

7–G   Make sure that students have one specific couple in mind as they write these sentences. To check their writing, have volunteers put some of their sentences on the board. Allow for peer correction.

7–H
7–I   Clarify the decision-making task as necessary. Have students repeat the *Helpful Language* after you. Give students several minutes to study the

descriptions of Gladys, Carlos, Peter, and Troy and to ask about anything they don't understand. Then give groups a time limit of ten minutes or so to complete the discussion and the writing activity.

7-J Have representatives from several groups write their sentences from 7–I on the board. Allow the groups time to exchange views.

EXTENSION ACTIVITIES: If students enjoyed the discussion in 7–H and would like to repeat the activity, this time choosing a match for a man, bring in three large magazine pictures of women and one of a man. Tape the pictures on the chalkboard. Underneath or next to each picture, write a brief description of the person, similar to those in 7–H. Then conduct the activity as in 7–H and 7–I above.

Students might enjoy reading ads placed by people looking for partners in the *Personals* section of a local newspaper or magazine. Have students read for a purpose. Perhaps they could find another suitable candidate for Gladys or one for themselves!

CROSS-CULTURAL FOCUS: Courtship customs in the U.S. might be discussed and then compared with those in students' countries. The presence or absence of dating, matchmakers, arranged marriages, dating services, Personal columns, and so on, can be discussed, to the degree that students' linguistic abilities permit.

7-K Students can fill in the questionnaire in class, if time permits, or as homework. Pairs could compare their answers, or you could lead a whole-class discussion to see how much or how little students agree on the various questions.

8 DIVIDE THE HOUSEHOLD CHORES

8-A Students can work individually or in pairs on this Warming Up activity, using their dictionaries if necessary. Have them write the appropriate letters next to the phrases.

If students could benefit from practice with present continuous, use these pictures to drill the structure.

Listening Drill
    YOU: She's washing the dishes.
STUDENTS: I!
    YOU: They're washing a car.
STUDENTS: F!

Speaking Drill
    YOU: What's the man doing in C?
STUDENTS: He's mopping the floor.
    YOU: What are the kids doing in J?
STUDENTS: They're doing the laundry.

8–B gives students additional written practice with present continuous.

8-B Refer students who need further work with the present continuous tense to the GRAMMAR APPENDIX, page 110.

8-C Students can work on this vocabulary exercise individually or in pairs, using their dictionaries, if necessary, or you as a ready resource.

8-D Go over Vlado's sentences with the class, perhaps writing *I like* _____, *I don't mind* _____, and *I hate* _____ on the board. If your students have an interest in grammar and terminology, point out that *walking, taking out,* and *cooking* are called gerunds here. Point out that some verbs are followed by gerunds (for example, *mind*); some by either gerunds or infinitives (for example, *like*, *hate*); and others only by infinitives (there are no examples here, but you could mention *plan, decide, want*, and so on).

Then have students get into pairs. Explain that one partner will talk while the other circles the appropriate face.

8-E   This activity, along with subsequent ones, is intended to get students thinking critically about the division of labor in their own household. 8–E specifically focuses students' attention on their past, when perhaps a more traditional definition of gender roles prevailed.

After students complete the grid, encourage them to share, compare, and evaluate information about their childhood and family roles. You might ask, "In your family, who did most of the household chores? Mother? Father? Female family members? Male family members?" Take a poll of students' responses. If you see a pattern to these responses, ask, "Why do you think this was the case in most of your families? Do families today divide the chores in a similar way? In the USA? In your country?"

CROSS-CULTURAL FOCUS: If students have the language ability, you might encourage them to voice their opinions on gender roles, househusbands, career wives, two-career families, and child care in day-care centers. Elicit cross-cultural comparisons if possible.

8-F   Refer students who need further work with the simple past tense to the Grammar Appendix, page 112.

8-G   This activity has pairs discussing the details of their answers for 8–E. Before

students begin sharing their answers, you may want to put the following chart on the board.

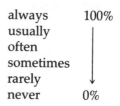

Point out that these frequency adverbs come before the verb. Some of them can also be found at the beginning or end of the sentence.

8-H   Clarify the decision-making task as necessary. Have students repeat the *Helpful Language* after you. Give groups a time limit of about fifteen minutes to complete their discussion and add up the total work time for each family member.

8-I   Before students begin sharing their ideas, put some language models on the board for them to follow, for example, *We decided that (mother) will work X hours. (She) will _____ and _____.*

8-J   *EXTENSION ACTIVITY:* Once students have written their first list of chores for the week, ask them to also list their other responsibilities for the week (for example, *Study! Go to class every day! Work on Tuesday and Thursday! Call home! Pay bills!*). Students can then make a weekly schedule and plot day by day, or even hour by hour, which chores and responsibilities they will take care of and when. Are there any they will have to postpone to a later date?

9 HELP OUT WITH FAMILY PROBLEMS

This problem is a relatively challenging and serious one. It gets students to talk and think about common difficulties of contemporary family life. The activities are designed to encourage students to consider how difficult situations can be eased or worked out not only by discussion among family members but also by seeking help from community organizations and services that are commonly available to people in the United States. Thus, this problem may serve as a way to introduce those students who may not be aware of community services to things such as counseling services and help lines.

Many individual and cultural factors come into play with a discussion about family problems. In some of the students' cultures, certain problems are not discussed outside the immediate family. Also, in some cultures, it may be a sign of weakness to talk about personal and family problems to others. In any case, there is a need to deal sensitively with the issues in this lesson.

9–A In this matching exercise, students may encounter new vocabulary such as *abuse* and *unemployment*. In most cases, the drawings should illustrate these new terms clearly. Nevertheless, before starting this activity, have ready some basic definitions or examples of words and expressions that may be new.

9–B Other kinds of family difficulties that students might suggest are day care; inadequate housing and high cost of housing; legal problems or problems with the police; in-laws, and specifically difficulties with aging grandparents who live with their married children; and homesickness. As for the *most serious* situations, those that involve health and physical well-being might be cited; however, there are no wrong answers here, and students are giving opinions relative to their own backgrounds and situations.

Concepts and structures of the family vary from culture to culture, so you should anticipate some different ideas from your students about family problems.

9–D Ideally there will be students in your class who disagree with one another about Ramon's idea that money can solve all his problems. Some students may point out, for example, that money can buy good medical care. Also, problems of divorce, drugs, unhappiness, and so on, are problems that both rich and poor people can have. If one of your students doesn't come up with the idea that money also *causes* problems, you may want to bring it up yourself!

9–E Additional practice with *should* and with modals in general is usually beneficial to all students. The use of *should* for giving advice is important in doing the subsequent activities (9–F through 9–J).

9–F One partner reads the situation. The other partner uses the advice phrase provided to give a suggestion with *should* or *shouldn't*, for example, "She should see a doctor." Encourage students to come up with some of their own suggestions for these situations.

9–G This activity provides hypothetical problem situations that involve (1) child abuse, (2) alcoholism, and (3) teen pregnancy. In small groups (you can also use pairs if you have a small class), have students choose one of four or more possible courses of action for each situation. Make it very clear to students that there are no right or wrong answers and that these are not real situations. If you feel that any of these "serious situations" are inappropriate for your class because of students' ages, situations, cultures, or religions, or because of your own sensitivity to the subject, skip over them.

9-I   If students need help writing their reasons, refer them to the *Helpful Language* on the following page. Other expressions are "Many people have this kind of problem," or "(_____/It) is a serious problem in our town," or "This help line can help a lot of people."

10   GIVE A GIFT

To introduce this lesson, bring in any store or gift order catalog as a visual aid to help students relate to the idea of catalog shopping. Ask if people in the class use catalogs to shop and, if so, for what sorts of things.

10-A   Students can work individually or in pairs to match the pictures with the names of the items. Help with the pronunciation of any new vocabulary item. Students can write the appropriate name under each item if they like. To check students' work, ask, "Which item costs twelve dollars? Which one(s) cost ten dollars?" and so on. This will also give students extra listening practice with prices.

10-B   Here students can express a personal preference about the items pictured while at the same time getting pronunciation practice.

EXTENSION ACTIVITY: Bring in some items from home: a tie, a piece of jewelry, a hat,

and so on. Have students describe them and give their opinions about them. You might want to introduce adverbs to amplify the adjectives, for example, "It's *extremely/very/ sort of/not* stylish."

10-E   This paired activity prepares students for the final decision-making task by having them think and talk about what gifts are appropriate for the five individuals given here. The reasons students give may focus on the qualities of the *gift*, for example, "(Because) It's useful," and/or on the qualities of the *person*, for example, "(Because) He (Jimmy) is smart and likes to read."

EXTENSION ACTIVITY: Have students try to recall a very special gift they received at some point in their lives and tell a partner about it. Why was it special? Who gave it to them? What was the occasion? Partners can then report back to the class.

10-G   Sentences with *because* and *so* involve combining clauses, which may be challenging for students. The practice provided by the Independent Grammar Study may be beneficial for all students.

QUIZ IDEA: You can give a sentence-completion quiz to reinforce and check students' ability to handle *because* and *so* together with new vocabulary. Write on the board or dictate the following (or similar) sentences for completion.

1. I want to buy the teddy bear because _____.

2. The watch is too expensive, so _____.

3. Billie wants to buy the hair dryer because _____.

4. Aunt Millie never wears cologne, so _____.

5. My sister is getting married, so _____.

Have students complete the sentences using the new vocabulary from 10–A and 10–C. (Students could refer to the dictionary definitions for the adjectives in 10–C in writing their sentences.) When finished, they can exchange papers and compare answers.

10–H   This culminating problem-solving task has students choose gifts for hypothetical relatives and a neighbor. Note that students write reasons for their choices in 10–I on the following page.

CROSS-CULTURAL FOCUS: Gift-giving is different from culture to culture. Ask your students about the main gift-giving occasions in their cultures. Are birthdays a big day for celebration and gift-giving? weddings? graduations?

10–K   Thank-you notes may not be as common in other cultures as they are for many people in the United States, so this activity can provide models for the kinds of notes students may want to write on occasion.

EXTENSION ACTIVITY: Encourage students to write a thank-you note of their own to a person or persons they know. Help them revise and edit as appropriate.

11   WORK OUT A FAMILY BUDGET

Money—students' attitudes toward it and their spending habits—is the theme of this lesson. You might choose to begin it in a humorous or dramatic way by pulling some money out of your pockets, making a comment, and eliciting students' reactions to your comment. Another motivational technique might be to play (or sing!) one of the many songs that have been written about money.

11–A   After discussing these proverbs with students, elicit similar ones from them in their languages (in translation). You could also introduce and discuss the proverbs "Money can't buy happiness" and "Money is the root of all evil" in this context.

After students have circled, either individually or in pairs, the free activities pictured, ask a sampling of students, "How many free activities did you find?" There will probably not be a consensus on this question, so use the disagreement as a stimulus for 11–B by saying, "OK. We'll discuss which ones are free in a minute, but first match the words in 11–B with the pictures."

11–B   Students can match the words and pictures on their own or with a partner by writing the words near the pictures. You might encourage students to help each other, use their dictionaries, or ask you about words that are unknown.

Once students know the names of the activities, they can begin discussing their costs. Encourage discussion and disagreement. A student may say, for example, "Dancing is free." Remain silent and noncommittal, allowing thinking time. Others may respond, "But dancing at the 21 Club is expensive!" The cost of other activities, likewise, may depend on a variety of factors (reading a book may be expensive if you buy it, but it's free if you get it from the library, and so on).

While students are exchanging opinions about the costs of the various activities, give them the help they need with using a gerund or gerund phrase as a subject. Explain that these words are formed from verbs but that they function as nouns here.

11–C   Refer students who need further work with gerunds as subjects to the GRAMMAR APPENDIX, page 116.

11-E   Before pairs begin this activity, bring the past tense question form with *did* to their attention. If students are unfamiliar with how to quote prices, refer them to the box on page 22 in Lesson 4.

You might point out in this context that while Americans sometimes discuss the costs of small, everyday purchases, they don't generally ask one another how much they paid for larger items such as cars, houses, or more expensive items of clothing. Nor are salaries usually discussed.

EXTENSION ACTIVITY: Helping students become familiar with stores in your area and making them aware of the benefits of comparison shopping in the U.S. would be appropriate goals in this context, if time permits and students express an interest. To sensitize students to the considerable difference in price that may be charged for the same item in various stores, give them the brand name of an item and have them telephone various stores to price the item (for example, an upscale department store, a moderately priced one, and a discount house). Give them the language they'll need for the phone calls.

How much is your (Sony cordless telephone)?

Could you please tell me the price of _____?

I'd like to price the _____.

Have students share their ideas of the best places to shop for various types of merchandise. Point out that prices are not the only indication of a "good" store; courteous service and a willingness to take back merchandise, for whatever the reason, are also important. The return policy that exists in most reputable stores in the U.S. might be stressed, as this is a concept that does not exist universally.

11-F   To warm students up for this categorizing activity, have them look at the items in 11-D and put them in these categories. Then give a time limit of ten minutes or so, and have students think of how they spent their money in the past month.

11-G   See if there is a consensus in the class about students' biggest and smallest expenditures. Allow comments or discussion to arise naturally; students should not be forced to talk about anything that feels too personal to them.

11-H   Clarify the decision-making task as necessary. Have students repeat the *Helpful Language* after you. Give the groups a time limit of ten to fifteen minutes to complete their discussion and fill out the Monthly Budget form.

11-J   Two writing options are given here. Students can choose one or do both. Those who do option A can share their writing with a partner instead of or before handing it in to you. Since option B is rather personal, tell students that they are writing only for themselves and that they will not have to hand in or share their budgets.

12 DECIDE ON APPROPRIATE SALARIES

12-A   Students can work individually or in pairs. They can either write the name of the job next to each picture or the letter of the picture next to the name of each job. Then ask, "What job does the person in *c* have?" Continue similarly with the remaining pictures. Clarify the terms *appropriate*, *salary*, *health food*, and *position*, if necessary.

EXTENSION ACTIVITIES: In pairs, have students write as many names of jobs as they can. Say "Stop" after several minutes. The pair with the most names wins a prize. You may want to have some students write the names on the board.

Or try a version of Twenty Questions. Have each student pick a job without disclosing it to anyone. One at a time, a student takes a turn and has the others guess her or his job using yes/no questions, for example, "Do you sit at a desk? Do you work with a lot of people?"

12-C   Some students may prefer to use some of their own ideas to complete the sentences. Point out that in conjoined sentences such as these, the same subject is generally not repeated after *and*.

12-D   The model shows how students can make personal comments about their jobs using *have to* and *can* (written practice with these verbs is on page 117 in the GRAMMAR APPENDIX. Note that the comments with *can* express a possibility, or positive aspect of the job, for example, "Chefs *can* be creative"; whereas the comments with *have to* express an obligation, or negative aspect of the job, for example, "Dishwashers have to stand up all day." Encourage students to use their own ideas too.

QUIZ IDEA: Have students look over the names of the jobs in 12-A and the "work" verbs and phrases from 12-C. After they close their books, write the following lists on the board.

1. scrub	a. money
2. chop	b. windows
3. take	c. tables
4. clear	d. employees
5. wash	e. guitar
6. play	f. vegetables
7. supervise	g. pots and pans

On their own paper, have students match the related words, for example, *scrub pots and pans*. Then ask them to write a complete sentence for each match, adding the appropriate employee and making all other necessary changes, for example, *A custodian washes windows*. (If it is too challenging for your students to supply the appropriate employee, these may also be listed in random order on the board: *dishwasher, business manager, busboy, chef, guitarist, custodian, cashier*.)

12-F   If students are unfamiliar with rank ordering, you may need to clarify the directions further by indicating that each job will have a different ranking: 1, 2, 3, and so on, to 7, with 1 being the most interesting in their opinions. Emphasize that there are no right or wrong answers; rather, the rankings depend on their own preferences. With both this activity and 12-G, it is important to sustain an open, nonjudgmental environment in which students can feel free to articulate their values and preferences.

CROSS-CULTURAL FOCUS: Ask students which jobs are considered good in their countries. You may want to help the discussion by pointing out that "good" jobs are usually associated with high *prestige* (respect) as well as good benefits and a high salary.

12-G   There are various ways to do this activity. If you feel students are comfortable reading through and marking the questionnaire on their own, you can circulate to answer questions, clarify any new terms, and exchange a few comments about their responses as they go along. A second alternative is to read through the items together one by one and then have students check the appropriate response before you go on to the next one. A third is to have partners read through the items together and then mark their own answers. At the end, when students share some of their responses with a partner or with the whole class, you can again point out how our different values express the things that are more important or less important to us.

12-H
12-I   This culminating activity has students playing the roles of co-owners of a health food cafeteria. Ultimately, each group needs to decide a dollar figure for the salary of each of the seven different positions. Ideally, group members will have a lively discussion about what salary is appropriate to the kinds of responsibilities involved in each position. They write reasons for their final choices in 12-I.

CROSS-CULTURAL FOCUS: In some cultures, salaries are discussed in terms of *monthly* salary. Help students who may think in these terms translate the yearly into monthly salaries. Final decisions, however, should be phrased in terms of yearly salaries.

EXTENSION ACTIVITY: Bring recent copies of the classified ads from your local paper to class. Distribute them to students and have students skim through the Help Wanted ads, noting job positions, responsibilities, and salaries. Then, as a class, have students compare these to the job positions at Sunrise Cafeteria.

13 PICK YOUR PERFECT VACATION

13-A   Have students look at the vacation ads. Ask, "Where do these tours take you?" As students come up with the answers (Montana, Egypt, Puerto Rico, East Africa), have volunteers point out the locations on a wall map or on a rough map you have sketched on the board. Then have students read the ads and circle the words that are new to them. Students can work in pairs to guess the meanings. Be sure to ask students what in the context helped them arrive at the meaning of a new word.

13-B   Give pairs a few minutes to discuss which holidays look most interesting. Then ask for volunteers to report on what their partners said. If you wish to preview the new vocabulary in 13-C at this point, ask, "Why does this place look interesting to you? What can you do there?"

13-C   To check students' writing, circulate while pairs are working and/or ask some pairs to write their sentences on the board. Students who have not written on the board can be called on to edit the work of their peers. Note that students' answers may vary.

13-D   Before assigning this activity, you might want to model the interview with a student, for example, "Jean-Luc, do you like to swim on vacation? Do you like to sleep a lot? Do you like to dance?" The target structure, *Do you like* + verb, could be written on the board, along with appropriate responses (*Yes, I do./No, I don't.*). Then ask pairs to interview each other for a few moments and fill in the blanks in the sentences.

EXTENSION ACTIVITY: Have students in pairs tell each other about a particularly memorable vacation they have taken; perhaps it was wonderful or disastrous. To prepare students for this activity, you might elicit from the class some good things that can happen on vacation as well as some bad things. Write these on the board. For example:

I/We saw fascinating things.

I/We relaxed, slept, and ate.

I fell in love.

I met some interesting people.

I/We lost my/our luggage.

I/We got lost.

I/We missed the train/plane.

I/We ran out of money.

The weather was terrible.

Ask partners to take notes as they listen to the story. Students can then be asked either to write the story of their partner's memorable vacation or retell it to the class.

13-E   This exercise is designed to get students to think more critically about advertising. You may want to prepare students beforehand by showing them some print ads for liquor, cigarettes, or cars and saying, for example, "Smoking looks romantic and fun in this ad. But what doesn't the ad tell you?" After asking students if they have any questions on the vocabulary in the box, have them work individually or in pairs to complete the task. Allow students to share their ideas.

13-F   For additional oral practice, ask students about the weather in their countries at various times of the year.

13-G   Refer students who need further work on the difference between *too* and *very* to the GRAMMAR APPENDIX, page 118.

13-H   *EXTENSION ACTIVITY:* Bring in copies of a current weather report from a local paper or from *USA Today*. Write three or four specific questions about today's or tomorrow's weather in your region and elsewhere and have students scan for the answers. Additional weather vocabulary can be dealt with in this context also.

QUIZ IDEA: Tell students to study the vocabulary in 13–A to 13–H in preparation for a dictation that will include many of these words and phrases. You could dictate several sentences or, better yet, a short, cohesive paragraph incorporating much of what students have learned. In this case, read the entire paragraph to students first and then dictate the text in natural groupings, pausing after each portion to allow time for writing. Finally, reread the paragraph at normal speed to allow students to check their work. For grading purposes, you may want to give one point for each correct section that students have written.

13-I
13-J   Clarify the decision-making task as necessary. Have students repeat the *Helpful Language* after you. Give the groups a time limit of about ten to fifteen minutes for their discussion and to complete the sentences in 13–J.

13-L   For extra practice with writing, have students first work in pairs on the Paris ad. Then ask them to write an ad for their native town or city, using their own paper and pictures. (This will work well as a homework assignment.) When students bring in their ads, pin them up on a wall or bulletin board.

14   DESIGN IN-FLIGHT UNIFORMS

14–A   This Warming Up activity can be done individually or in pairs. Students can either use dictionaries or ask you questions when they have difficulty. Students for whom most of this vocabulary is brand-new should probably be encouraged to write the names of the items near the pictures. Ask students if they can think of any clothing items not pictured here. They might come up with dress, suit, coat, hat, gloves, shoes, and socks.

14–B   Give pairs a few minutes to discuss their favorite clothes. Then ask for volunteers to report on what their partners said.

14–C   Students can work on this activity either individually or in pairs. To check students' work, you can monitor them as they work, have volunteers write their sentences on the board when all have finished, or, with more advanced classes, have students read their sentences aloud.

EXTENSION ACTIVITIES: To reinforce the vocabulary presented thus far via a listening comprehension task, tell students that you are going to describe what someone in the class is wearing and that they should try to guess who that person is. (Having the class sit in a circle for this activity would be optimal.) Then say, for example, (without looking at the student in question), "Someone is wearing a black jacket and a printed skirt. Who is it?" Having students write their answers instead of shouting them will give slower students some thinking time. Asking students to then hold up their written answers will give you some feedback as to how well individuals are comprehending. Be sure to repeat the description for those who need it. Continue in this vein with several more students. (The same thing can be done by hanging pictures of people wearing various types of clothing on the board and writing names beneath the pictures.)

To reinforce the vocabulary presented in 14–A and 14–C via a speaking task, put students in pairs or threes and have them, in turn, describe what a mystery person in the class is wearing while the others name the student (as above). Another game focusing on oral production involves more movement and works as follows: Have students form two circles with the same number of students in each. One circle should be inside the other. While the outer circle moves right, the inner one moves left. Students should be instructed to look carefully at the clothes of those in the other circle as they are passing. When you say, "Stop! Turn around!" students should get back-to-back with a partner from the other circle. They should then try to tell their partner what he or she is wearing. After you have given the pairs a minute or so to talk back-to-back, say, "OK. Turn around and see if you're right!" Stop the game after five minutes or before students begin to tire of it.

14–D   Refer students who need further work with the order of adjectives to the GRAMMAR APPENDIX, page 119.

14–E   Before pairs begin this activity, have them look at the adjectives in the box. Preteach any unknown words or, better yet, elicit examples or definitions from students who do know the meanings. Then model the dialog with a student, for example, "Salima, do you like the turtleneck top?"

CROSS-CULTURAL FOCUS: Teach students how to compliment each other on their clothes. Tell them that compliments on clothing are common in the United States, especially among women. Teach them a few forms for complimenting as well as appropriate responses to a compliment.

What a (great, nice, pretty) _____!

That's a (beautiful, good-looking) _____.

I really like your _____.

Thank you!

Thank you. It's new.

Oh, thanks. I've had it a long time.

Then you might ask students to stand up, move about the classroom, and compliment each other on their clothing.

QUIZ IDEA: Tell students to study the vocabulary in 14–A through 14–E. Tell them to prepare for an oral quiz in which you will show them pictures of people and they must describe what the people are wearing in as much detail as possible. They should also be ready to give their opinions about the clothing, using adjectives from 14–E. Students could be quizzed either individually (during your office hours or while other students are writing) or, if your class is small, in front of other students.

14–F Have students share their ratings with their classmates. More advanced students can explain their reasons.

14–G Clarify the decision-making task as necessary. Have students repeat the *Helpful Language* after you. Give the groups a time limit of fifteen minutes or so to complete their discussion, the drawing, and the uniform description.

14–I You might want to have students share their memos with classmates who were not in their group. If students want to vote on the best design, pin one memo from each group on the bulletin board. Allow students to look them over, summarize the uniform ideas on the board, and call a vote.

15 PLAN A CLASS TRIP

The objective of this lesson is for students to work together to plan a class trip. If you are unable to actually follow through with a class trip, we recommend that you do not use this lesson.

15–A This Warming Up activity can be done individually or in pairs. Suggest to students that they write the names of the places under the pictures. Allow them to hear and practice the pronunciations of these words at some point.

15–B This exercise can start students thinking about what facilities their local community offers for cultural, recreational, and educational purposes. Other places in your community may include the following: skating or ice rinks, clubs or discos, libraries, theaters, other museums, recreation centers, newspaper offices, public TV stations, state fairgrounds, and restaurants. You may wish to talk about the locations of some of the facilities in 15–A at this point and have students give their evaluations of the places. Students may appreciate hearing about some of your favorite places.

15–C Go over a few examples with the whole class before instructing students to see how many true sentences they can make from this chart. Students can draw lines as in the example to remember the sentences they've created, but some students may prefer to write the sentences out. Give students five to ten minutes for this activity. Encourage them to ask you questions about vocabulary that they need as they proceed. Learning vocabulary as the communicative need for certain words or phrases arises can be very effective.

Or, you can make this activity into a game by telling pairs, "You have five minutes to write as many true sentences as possible. The pair with the most sentences will win!" The pair that wrote the most sentences should read them aloud to the class slowly, stopping after each. Allow the other students to act as judges and to decide when a point can be given for a sentence. You may decide to award a small, nonsense prize to the winning pair.

15-D   Tell pairs that they have five minutes to dictate three sentences to each other. Remind them either to self-correct or to correct their partner's work.

QUIZ IDEA: Have students study the chart as homework to prepare for a dictation based on the chart the next class period.

15-E   Refer students who need further work with infinitives of purpose to the GRAMMAR APPENDIX, page 120.

15-F   Students will be compiling information here, and to supplement what they come up with, it will be necessary for you to come to class prepared with the names of the relevant local places, their locations, their approximate distances from school, and any costs involved. Copies of a local map as well as the local phone directory could be helpful. Work with students on the first one or two items on the grid to be sure they understand the activity.

15-G   Give students a time limit for this "mixer" activity. If you feel students are

capable of and would benefit from making telephone calls to find out information, provide them with a phone book or telephone numbers and give each group the task of calling one place to get or verify information.

15-H   Keep groups as in 15–F. Go over the *Helpful Language* with them and then set a time limit for the completion of the proposed itinerary.

15-I   This sharing does not need to be detailed or exhaustive at this time because students will be discussing their proposed itineraries and reaching a whole-class decision after completing 15–K (see below).

15-J   Refer students who need further work with *will* to the GRAMMAR APPENDIX, page 121.

15-K   After collecting students' memos, select one from each group. Look them over and then share their contents with the class (either by summarizing the proposed itineraries on the board, by photocopying or mimeographing each group's plans, or by transferring them to overhead transparencies). Ask students to vote on which plan they find most feasible and interesting. Vote on a suitable day for the outing. Once a destination has been selected, more in-class work can be done in preparation for the trip; students can do some related reading (perhaps there are brochures available), write questions about things they want to find out, and so on.

INDEX